Chinese Military Power

*Report of an Independent Task Force
Sponsored by the
Council on Foreign Relations
Maurice R. Greenberg Center
for Geoeconomic Studies*

Harold Brown, Chair
Joseph W. Prueher, Vice Chair
Adam Segal, Project Director

The Council on Foreign Relations is dedicated to increasing America's understanding of the world and contributing ideas to U.S. foreign policy. The Council accomplishes this mainly by promoting constructive debates and discussions, clarifying world issues, and publishing *Foreign Affairs,* the leading journal on global issues. The Council is host to the widest possible range of views, but an advocate of none, though its research fellows and Independent Task Forces do take policy positions.

THE COUNCIL TAKES NO INSTITUTIONAL POSITION ON POLICY ISSUES AND HAS NO AFFILIATION WITH THE U.S. GOVERNMENT. ALL STATEMENTS OF FACT AND EXPRESSIONS OF OPINION CONTAINED IN ALL ITS PUBLICATIONS ARE THE SOLE RESPONSIBILITY OF THE AUTHOR OR AUTHORS.

The Council will sponsor an Independent Task Force when (1) an issue of current and critical importance to U.S. foreign policy arises, and (2) it seems that a group diverse in backgrounds and perspectives may, nonetheless, be able to reach a meaningful consensus on a policy through private and nonpartisan deliberations. Typically, a Task Force meets between two and five times over a brief period to ensure the relevance of its work.

Upon reaching a conclusion, a Task Force issues a report, and the Council publishes its text and posts it on the Council website. Task Force reports can take three forms: (1) a strong and meaningful policy consensus, with Task Force members endorsing the general policy thrust and judgments reached by the group, though not necessarily every finding and recommendation; (2) a report stating the various policy positions, each as sharply and fairly as possible; or (3) a "Chairman's Report," where Task Force members who agree with the Chairman's report may associate themselves with it, while those who disagree may submit dissenting statements. Upon reaching a conclusion, a Task Force may also ask individuals who were not members of the Task Force to associate themselves with the Task Force report to enhance its impact. All Task Force reports "benchmark" their findings against current administration policy in order to make explicit areas of agreement and disagreement. The Task Force is solely responsible for its report. The Council takes no institutional position.

For further information about the Council or this Task Force, please write the Council on Foreign Relations, 58 East 68th Street, New York, NY 10021, or call the Director of Communications at (212) 434-9400. Visit our website at www.cfr.org.

CONTENTS

FOREWORD

During the half century of the Cold War, American perspectives on the U.S.-Soviet military balance tended to extremes, alternating between frequent alarmism and occasional triumphalism. At times, inflated assessments of Soviet power and excessive pessimism about U.S. strength undercut efforts to improve ties between the two countries. In other instances, unwarranted euphoria about U.S. strength encouraged passivity in the face of a Soviet Union that actually was growing stronger. Strong feelings on all sides of the discussion politicized the domestic debate, with ill effect for U.S. policymaking.

The aim of this report is to provide a nonpartisan and pragmatic approach to assessing the trends in Chinese military modernization so as to avoid the wide and unfounded swings that characterized similar judgments about the Soviets during the Cold War.

This Task Force report has been released as part of the work of the Maurice R. Greenberg Center for Geoeconomic Studies. The goal of the center is to mix the study of foreign policy and economics. As part of this process, the Task Force report focuses not only on the Chinese military establishment, but also on the larger economic, political, and technological context shaping Chinese military modernization.

In late 2001, I spoke with former Secretary of Defense Harold Brown and Admiral (Ret.) Joseph W. Prueher about forming an Independent Task Force to assess the current capabilities of the Chinese military and establish milestones for judging the future evolution of Chinese military power. Dr. Brown and Admiral Prueher both have a long and esteemed history of involvement in this important issue. They, along with the expert members of the Task Force, have developed measures that will allow observers of Chinese military modernization to determine the degree to which changes in the quantity and in the quality of China's military power may threaten the interests of the United States, its allies, and its friends.

This Task Force finds that although China is in the midst of a comprehensive modernization program, the Chinese military is at least two decades behind the United States in terms of military technology and capability. Moreover, the Task Force judges that if the United States continues to dedicate significant resources to improving its military forces, as expected, the balance between the United States and China, both globally and in Asia, is likely to remain decisively in America's favor beyond the next twenty years.

The Task Force notes that the Taiwan Strait is an area of near-term military concern. For the next decade, a focal point of Chinese military development will likely remain achieving the ability to influence Taiwan's choices about its political future or, failing that, preventing Taiwan from achieving formal independence.

Although U.S. forces would ultimately prevail in a military crisis or conflict, Beijing might be able to impose serious risks and costs on the U.S. military if the United States concluded that it was necessary to commit air and naval forces to battle with China in defense of Taiwan. Any conflict across the Taiwan Strait would have an extremely adverse impact on the strategic landscape in Asia, regardless of the military outcome. Therefore, the most critical aim of U.S. strategy in the cross-strait situation must be to deter and minimize the chances that such a crisis will occur.

The Task Force recommends specific milestones to gauge the pace of Chinese military modernization as China acquires limited power-projection capabilities. The Task Force has also developed indicators that would signal major shifts away from these current priorities.

My deepest admiration and appreciation go to Dr. Brown and Admiral Prueher for their excellent leadership in this critical project. I am grateful to Adam Segal, project director, for his expertise in draftsmanship and independence of thought. Thanks also to Council Military Fellow Colonel Christopher Miller, U.S. Air Force, who served skillfully as project coordinator during the first year of the Task Force.

Leslie H. Gelb
President
Council on Foreign Relations

ACKNOWLEDGMENTS

The Council on Foreign Relations was very fortunate that Harold Brown agreed to serve as chair and that Joseph W. Prueher acted as vice chair of the Task Force. They guided the Task Force with intelligence, grace, and aplomb through an extremely complicated subject and a very long process. I feel extremely privileged and honored to have had the opportunity to work with them.

I am enormously grateful to the members of the Task Force for all their hard work and their input into the report. Given the large size of the Task Force and the diversity of opinions and experiences, I thank all the members for their good humor and collegiality. John Deutch, Winston Lord, and Susan Shirk served skillfully as the chairs of the technological, political, and economic subcommittees, respectively, and did much important work to sharpen the focus and findings of the Task Force.

A number of members as well as individuals from outside the Task Force made presentations to the Task Force, and I thank them for their important contributions. Kenneth Allen, Kurt Campbell, Thomas Christensen, Bernard Cole, Karl Eikenberry, David Finkelstein, John Frankenstein, Bates Gill, Paul Heer, Deborah Lehr, Eric McVadon, James Mulvenon, Robert Ross, Bruce Russett, David Shambaugh, Richard Solomon, Mark Stokes, Michael Swaine, Stephen Voth, and Dennis Wilder all provided critical information on specific issue areas.

This report would not have been possible without the dedication of Benjamin Brake. He produced excellent rapporteur's reports, took part in the meetings, and facilitated the overall smooth working of the Task Force. During 2001–2002, Colonel Christopher Miller, Council on Foreign Relations military fellow, U.S. Air Force, acted as project director and was instrumental in keeping the Task Force on track and on target. Lee Feinstein, deputy director of the Studies Program at the Council, provided able support throughout the process.

The generous financial support of the Arthur Ross Foundation allowed the Task Force to complete its work in an efficient and timely manner.

Finally, I thank Council President Leslie H. Gelb for his consistent encouragement and sage advice. My early discussions with Les during the planning stages were instrumental in sharpening the intellectual focus and structure of the Task Force.

Adam Segal

EXECUTIVE SUMMARY

The People's Republic of China (PRC) is currently engaged in a comprehensive military modernization. This report addresses the state of China's military capabilities, assesses the current capabilities of the People's Liberation Army (PLA), and establishes milestones for judging the evolution of Chinese military power over the next twenty years. These assessments and milestones will provide policymakers and the public with a pragmatic and nonpartisan approach to measuring the development of Chinese military power. They will allow observers of Chinese military modernization to determine the degree to which changes in the quantity and quality of China's military power may threaten the interests of the United States, its allies, and its friends, as well as how the United States should adjust and respond politically, diplomatically, economically, and militarily to China's military development.

The report issues a double warning: first, against overreaction to the large scale of China's military modernization program; and second, against underreaction based on the relative backwardness of the People's Liberation Army compared with U.S. military power. Attributing to the PLA capabilities it does not have and will not attain for many years could result in the misallocation of scarce resources. Overreaction could lead the United States to adopt policies and undertake actions that become a self-fulfilling prophecy, provoking an otherwise avoidable antagonistic relationship that will not serve long-term U.S. interests. Underreaction, on the other hand, might allow China to someday catch unawares the United States or its friends and allies in Asia.

In analyzing the likely evolution of PLA capabilities, this report not only describes development processes and institutional, technological, personnel, doctrinal, and other systemic issues internal to the Chinese military establishment; it also takes into account the economic, political, strategic, and technological context shaping modernization. This larger context motivates, structures, and, at times, constrains military modernization as much as the factors emerging from within the Chinese military.

FINDINGS

The Council on Foreign Relations Independent Task Force on Chinese Military Power finds that the People's Republic of China is pursuing a deliberate and focused course of military modernization but that it is at least two decades behind the United States in terms of military technology and capability. Moreover, if the United States continues to dedicate significant resources to improving its military forces, as expected, the balance between the United States and China, both globally and in Asia, is likely to remain decisively in America's favor beyond the next twenty years.

There are multiple drivers of China's military modernization. The PLA, along with the People's Armed Police and the People's Militia, helps maintain domestic stability and ensure regime security. China is developing limited power-projection capabilities to deal with a range of possible conflict scenarios along its periphery, especially in maritime areas. The PLA is acquiring military capabilities designed to defend Chinese sovereignty and territorial interests and to pose a credible threat to Taiwan in order to influence Taiwan's choices about its political future; or, failing that, to prevent Taiwan from achieving political independence. These capabilities are also intended to deter, delay, or complicate U.S. efforts to intervene on behalf of Taiwan. In addition, military modernization is expected to enhance China's international prestige.

China is a regional power, and the Task Force does not envisage China becoming a globally committed military power in the next two decades. If current trends continue (e.g., if Japan continues to eschew a role as a major regional military power), the Task Force expects that China will become the predominant military power among the nations of East Asia. China's current force structure and doctrine provide effective "defense-in-depth" against any effort to invade and seize Chinese territory. The PLA possesses power projection across land borders against smaller regional powers and the ability to dislodge those powers from nearby disputed land and maritime territories. In the next two decades, the Task Force expects China will acquire a greater capability to hold and seize such territories against combined regional forces.

However, the Task Force also notes that although China will have the enduring advantage of proximity to Asia, Beijing has traditionally been weakest and the United States has traditionally been strongest in the maritime, aerospace, and technological dimensions of military power. Consequently, although China is already the strongest continental military power in East Asia and destined to become an even greater power beyond its littoral borders, a sustained and robust U.S. naval and air presence can offset the ability of Beijing to leverage future military capabilities into a real advantage against U.S. and allied interests in the Asia-Pacific region over the next twenty years, if not longer.

The Taiwan Strait is an area of near-term military concern. Current Chinese policy is to avoid a military confrontation if at all possible. For the next decade, a focal point of Chinese military development will likely remain achieving the ability to influence Taiwan's choices about its political future or, failing that, to prevent Taiwan from achieving formal independence. Here, China is more likely to use new technologies and asymmetric strategies, not to invade Taiwan outright but rather to achieve political goals such as forcing the resumption of political dialogue between the two sides on the mainland's terms. In a crisis, China may also use its military to counter Taiwan's economic prosperity by blockade, laying mines in the Taiwan Strait, or other means. Moreover, Beijing could decide to utilize force against Taiwan under certain circumstances even if the balance of forces across the strait favored the United States and Taiwan.

The PLA currently has the ability to undertake intensive, short-duration air, missile, and naval attacks on Taiwan, as well as more prolonged air and naval attacks. The efficacy of either scenario would be highly dependent on Taiwan's political and military response, and especially on any actions taken by the United States and Japan.

Although U.S. forces would ultimately prevail in a military crisis or conflict, Beijing might be able to impose serious risks and costs on the U.S. military if the United States concluded that it was necessary to commit air and naval forces to battle with China in defense of Taiwan. Sovremenny-class destroyers armed with Sunburn (SS-N-22) antiship missiles and Kilo-class submarines armed with wake-homing torpedoes—plus the almost two dozen older submarines China could put to sea—could slow the intervention of a naval task force.

Any conflict across the Taiwan Strait would have an extremely adverse impact on the strategic landscape in Asia, regardless of the military outcome. Therefore, the most critical aim of U.S. strategy in the cross-strait situation must be to deter and minimize the chances that such a crisis will occur. Taiwan is fundamentally a political issue, and any effective strategy must coordinate military measures designed to deter with diplomatic efforts so as to reassure both China and Taiwan credibly that their worst fears will not materialize. For U.S. policy toward Taiwan, this means providing Taiwan with the weapons and assistance deemed necessary for the creation of a robust defense capability and not making a deal with Beijing behind Taipei's back. For U.S. policy toward China, this means maintaining the clear ability and willingness to counter an application of military force against Taiwan while conveying to Beijing a credible U.S. commitment to not support Taiwan's taking unilateral steps toward de jure independence.

The Task Force expects that the United States will continue to possess overwhelming dominance over China's nuclear forces for the foreseeable future. China, however, is improving the survivability of its small, retaliatory, "countervalue" deterrent force. China's nuclear arsenal will likely expand in number and sophistication over the next ten to twenty years. Although the Task Force is uncertain about the specific impact of U.S. missile defense plans on Chinese nuclear modernization in terms of numbers and force deployment, we believe that China will do whatever it can to ensure that a U.S. missile defense system cannot negate its ability to launch and deliver a retaliatory second strike.

Executive Summary

THE CONTEXT OF MILITARY MODERNIZATION

The Task Force's assessment of the People's Liberation Army is rooted in a multidimensional analysis of the economic, technological, and political context of military modernization.

Chinese spending on military modernization rose throughout the 1990s. As announced in March 2003 at the National People's Congress, the official PLA budget is RMB 185.3 billion (U.S. $22.4 billion). This year's announced increase of 9.6 percent in military expenditures, however, was the lowest rise in thirteen years, and the official defense budgets have remained relatively small in terms of their shares of gross domestic product (1.6 percent in 2002) and total government expenditure (8.5 percent in 2002).

Estimates by foreign analysts of the PLA budget vary between two to twelve times the published official figure. Higher estimates—$80 billion and upwards—tend to adopt a method of accounting (the use of purchasing power parity) that gives very imprecise results. The Task Force notes that actual expenditures are certainly higher than the official number. The published PLA budget excludes several important categories of spending, such as conversion subsidies; research and development (R&D) costs; support of the People's Armed Police; cost of weapons purchased from abroad; proceeds from PLA commercial ventures; PLA foreign arms sales revenue; and operations and maintenance costs that are shared by local civilian governments. In any event, dollar figures for military expenditures are hardly meaningful in a developing economy where the exchange rate is fixed by the government, where military personnel costs are not set by economic criteria, and where expenditures are so mixed between *renminbi*, the domestic currency, and imports that neither purchasing power parity—even if calculated separately for each class of expenditure—nor exchange rates are a good measure.

With this caution, the Task Force estimates Chinese defense spending may be closer to two to three times higher than the official figure. This would place China's $44 billion to $67 billion in a range comparable to the $65 billion spent by Russia, the $43 billion spent by Japan, and the $38 billion spent by the United Kingdom.

Although China's advancement in some areas of commercial technology is impressive and China has emerged in recent years as a highly efficient manufacturing center and an increasingly powerful competitor in global markets, converting economic to military power will proceed more slowly. China's abilities to develop, produce, and, most important, integrate indigenously sophisticated military systems are limited. China is advancing less rapidly in developing military technology than in the application of certain commercial technologies because the system of innovation and acquisition, unlike in the civilian economy, remains the province of the PLA, the defense establishment bureaucracy, and state-owned enterprises whose productivity has lagged behind their nonmilitary and non–state-owned counterparts.

China is trying to offset its weakness in military technology by purchasing advanced technologies from other countries. Such purchases, however, will fall well short of compensating for domestic shortfalls. China has been cut off from all U.S. and European military suppliers since an arms and defense technology embargo was imposed in 1989 in response to the Tiananmen tragedy. Today the Task Force judges that the continuation of such an embargo is warranted because it will likely slow the pace of China's weapons modernization. A U.S.-only embargo, however, would have less impact. Consequently, it should be a U.S. foreign policy priority to maintain common ground with other major arms suppliers, perhaps fashioned around a shared commitment not to enhance the PLA's power-projection capabilities, while maintaining an export control regime that does not unnecessarily harm U.S. commercial engagement with China.

China's military modernization takes place against the backdrop of much broader changes in China's economy, society, and politics. For the foreseeable future, China will be preoccupied with domestic challenges—ensuring a smooth political succession; mitigating the dangers arising from the massive burden of nonperforming loans and a potential banking crisis; reforming state-owned enterprises; modernizing the legal system; curbing rising unemployment; ameliorating growing social and regional inequality; combating rampant official corruption; improving the environment; dealing with AIDS, SARS, and other public health crises; and dampening popular unrest. To address these domestic concerns, China's leaders need a peaceful international environment in general and good relations with the United States in particular. These needs and priorities of China offer the United States the potential to influence diplomatically both China's plans for military modernization and its policies relating to the threat of the use of force.

Furthermore, the Task Force believes that in spite of China's impressive growth rate in military spending over many years, the likelihood of ever-increasing demands for government funding in areas other than military development will constrain its pace of military modernization in the long term. China's armed forces must compete for resources and attention with social security, education, public health, science and technology, and large-scale public works projects. Although improving, the ability of the central government to collect fiscal revenue still is limited. With growing resource demands, any economic downturn will sharpen the competition between military and nonmilitary spending. These factors will limit, but not by themselves determine, the rate of China's military modernization.

METHODOLOGY

This report is the product of an intensive project that lasted more than a year. The Task Force convened ten times during this period. Scholars and experts provided comprehensive presentations on all the services of the PLA, information warfare, civil-military relations, China's national security environment, the PLA budget process, and Chinese defense industries, as well as on the political and military situation across the Taiwan Strait. In addition, three subgroups met separately to analyze the political, economic, and technological contexts of military modernization. These subgroups reported their findings to the full Task Force.

Building an analytic framework for evaluating Chinese military power is difficult. The further into the future we peer, the harder it is to predict capabilities and intentions. We can reach relatively well-informed judgments about PLA capabilities in 2008; similar judgments about 2018 are highly speculative; and comparing PRC to U.S. capabilities in 2028 is still more difficult.

These difficulties are compounded because of the relative lack of transparency of the Chinese defense establishment. The direction in which the Chinese military appears to be moving is easier to determine than the rate at which it progresses given information in the public domain. Chinese doctrinal writing, declared budget priorities, arms purchases, training innovations, and reform of the personnel management systems provide a fairly good picture of the capabilities the PLA hopes to develop and the types of wars it wants to be able to fight and win. The speed at which the PLA is able to travel down this road is another, and much less certain, matter.

The Task Force is aware of the problem of "mirror imaging"— the tendency to equate a potential enemy's situation with one's own, whether strategically, organizationally, culturally, or materially. The United States must not limit its assessment of potential Chinese capabilities to traditional U.S. plans for war. The PLA may try to solve problems in a manner considered unlikely or unsatisfactory by U.S. defense planners.

Comparing the backwardness of the PLA with the United States military is not the most fruitful analytical approach, given the distinctive political and strategic concerns of the Chinese leadership. Rather, the Task Force has tried to place potential PRC military capabilities in the context of their intended uses. In the case of Taiwan, the ends to which Beijing might apply force may well involve political pressure and potential coercive actions short of actual war fighting. PRC decisions to use force might be based on calculations other than (or in addition to) a simple assessment of the quantity and quality of U.S., Taiwanese, and PRC forces. It is also important to assess PLA capabilities relative to those of other Asian militaries, rather than to U.S. forces alone.

It is likewise difficult and risky to reach conclusions about Chinese strategic and political intentions from PLA military developments. The Task Force cautions against making a direct link between what the PLA thinks and does and what the civilian Chinese leadership intends. We do suggest some indicators of future military capabilities to watch. These capabilities may offer insights into intentions, but the capabilities of the Chinese military cannot be automatically mapped onto the intentions of the civilian leadership.

This Task Force focused on military issues. It has not addressed in detail the future evolution of Sino-American relations, which will help set the context of Chinese military planning. Political factors—in China, the United States, and Taiwan—will determine the nature of the bilateral relationship. The political implications of China's military modernization will depend as much on the policies of the United States and China's neighbors as on the military balance itself.

KEY UNCERTAINTIES

Although the Task Force does believe that U.S. forces could ultimately determine the military result of a direct conflict with China in any theater or at any level of escalation for at least the next twenty years, the outcome of any military conflict is never completely predictable. This uncertainty is heightened in the case of a potential conflict over Taiwan. Determining a "victor" in such a conflict would depend on political will in China, Taiwan, and the United States; Taiwan's military and political response; the U.S. military and political response; and public opinion in all three societies. In any case, the possibility that China could contest U.S. military influence successfully raises larger questions about the extent to which a potential U.S.-China conflict would be contained or might instead escalate to a wider geographic stage and to less restricted forms of warfare.

The Task Force spent considerable time discussing the situation across the Taiwan Strait, its role as a driver of Chinese military modernization, and its relationship to China's current and future strategic objectives. Some participants of the Task Force see China's approach to the Taiwan issue as a manifestation of a larger and more strategically ominous trend—the emergence of a China whose notions of regional expansion could put it on a collision course with American interests and commitments. Other participants, however, maintain a distinction between the Taiwan issue and the larger regional strategic interests called to mind by concerns over China as a "rising power" or potential "peer competitor" of the United States, and they challenge the assumption that a "great power" clash between the United States and China is all but historically foreordained. In either case, although the proper handling of the Taiwan issue cannot guarantee that a larger strategic confrontation between the United States and China will be avoided, the mishandling of the Taiwan issue could greatly accelerate movement toward such a confrontation.

The ability of the United States to influence the pace and scale of Chinese military modernization is also uncertain. Chinese military developments are substantially determined by what is happening within China, by the technical and financial resources available to the regime, and by Beijing's foreign policy priorities and external threat perceptions. Actions by the United States affect these perceptions, especially with regard to relations across the Taiwan Strait, the pace of U.S. military modernization, and U.S. missile defense plans.

The Task Force's projection about China as the predominant East Asian military power is based on the assumption that the other major regional powers—especially Japan—will continue their current military development trajectories. But an international or domestic crisis could fundamentally alter the security environment, threat perceptions, and defense spending of China's neighbors. Current events on the Korean Peninsula provide the most immediate example; a nuclear North Korea could strongly influence Japanese debates over revisions to Article IX of Japan's Constitution, the future size and role of the Japanese Self-Defense Forces, and the pursuit of a nuclear option that in turn would have a major effect on Chinese military programs.

Current Chinese strategic objectives reflect a political consensus within the leadership. The recent leadership succession is unlikely to change core strategic goals at least in the near term, especially with Jiang Zemin retaining the chairmanship of the Central Military Commission. That said, over the longer term, civil-military relations and the larger political context might change substantially. A liberalizing China may eventually mean a more pacific foreign policy, especially with regard to Taiwan, but a China undergoing reform might also pursue its sovereignty concerns more confidently. Political instability might delay or derail military modernization; it might also provoke a diversionary military conflict as a way to restore domestic political support.

RECOMMENDATIONS

Recommendation 1: Monitor the development of specific capabilities in order to gauge the pace of Chinese military modernization.

The current trajectory of Chinese military modernization reflects the PLA's shift from a military with a continental orientation requiring large land forces for "in-depth" defense to a military with a combined continental and maritime orientation requiring a smaller, more mobile, and more technologically advanced "active peripheral defense" capability. The Chinese military is acquiring new weapons platforms and has reformed doctrine and training to allow the PLA to project power farther away from its shores and to defend those forward-deployed forces from various forms of attack, including aircraft, submarine, and missile.

As the PLA moves from its current capabilities toward its future aspirations, the Task Force recommends that the following key indicators be used to help gauge the pace at which the Chinese military is modernizing. The indicators are grouped in five categories: command, control, communications, computers, intelligence, surveillance, and reconnaissance (C^4ISR); joint operations; precision strikes; combat support; and training.

C^4ISR

- Launch and maintenance of C^4ISR satellites able to provide real-time surveillance and expanded battle management capabilities
- Acquisition of airborne warning and control
- Development and use of unmanned aerial vehicles
- Development of Chinese information operations able to degrade U.S. intelligence, surveillance, and reconnaissance systems

Joint Operations

- Improvements in the ability to coordinate and execute multiservice exercises and joint operations in the various battle space dimensions (land, air, sea, electromagnetic spectrum, and outer space)
- Development of better air defense capabilities, including the integration of more advanced surface-to-air missiles like the SA-10
- The reorganization (or even abolition) of China's seven military regions (basically administrative entities) that would quickly enable the establishment of joint war zone commands (the near equivalent of theater of operations in the U.S. military)
- Improvements in communication architectures that enable war zone commanders to coordinate the movements and actions of major units across current military region boundaries
- An increase in the number of command post exercises in which officers from different military regions and services practice joint command-and-control activities

Precision Strikes

- Improvement in targeting technologies, especially over-the-horizon targeting
- Development of stealthy, long-range cruise missiles
- Increased ability to use U.S., European, or future indigenous global positioning systems to improve the accuracy of short-range ballistic missiles or other munitions

- Development and use of precision-guided munitions
- Training with antiship missiles by the People's Liberation Army Air Force (PLAAF) and/or the People's Liberation Army Navy–Air Force (PLANAF)
- Development of decoys, penetration aids, and other counters to missile defense measures

Combat Support
- Improvements to the recently established military region–based "joint" logistics system whereby it truly becomes capable of providing combat sustainability within the context of a war zone, not merely providing administrative peacetime logistic support within a military region
- Development of in-flight refueling and airborne command-and-control capabilities
- Moderate increase in airlift ability—beyond the three divisions in the airborne corps
- Moderate increase in sea-lift capabilities

Training
- Increases in the frequency of training missions with SU-27, SU-30, and other advanced aircraft; in the number of hours pilots train in advanced fighters; and in the sortie rates that can be generated with these aircraft
- Improved execution of training exercises that involve joint ground and air units

In addition, given China's critical dependence on Russia for weapons and defense technologies as well as spare parts, repairs, and logistics, the development of an indigenous capacity to manufacture the systems and weapons China now purchases from Russia would be an important sign of progress in Chinese defense industries. This is especially true in the case of technologies involved in fourth-generation fighters, over-the-horizon radars, air defense and air-to-air missiles, sophisticated surface combatants, and advanced submarines.

Recommendation 2: Look for signs that China's military development trajectory has changed significantly.

Although the Task Force has laid out the most probable development trajectory of the PLA over the next twenty years, it realizes that this trajectory may shift.

The Task Force developed the indicators listed in the previous recommendation as a means to gauge the pace of a development trajectory focused on acquiring limited power-projection capabilities. The indicators that would represent major shifts away from these current priorities, greatly changing the nature of the Chinese modernization program, include:

- A crash program to build more amphibious warfare ships;
- Rapid expansion of the People's Liberation Army Navy (PLAN) marine force;
- Significant efforts to expand both airborne and airlift capabilities;
- Acquisition of SU-27s and SU-30s by the PLANAF or the expanded operation of PLAAF forces over water;
- The assignment of PLAN and PLAAF officers to senior PLA posts;
- A dramatic increase in the pace of submarine force modernization, including the construction and deployment of more Type-094 ballistic missile submarines;
- Major increases in intercontinental ballistic missile warheads by launcher numbers or by the development of multiple independently targeted reentry vehicles beyond those that might be necessary to maintain a Chinese nuclear second-strike capability in the face of U.S. missile defenses;
- Formal changes in the no-first-use (NFU) doctrine on nuclear weapons;
- Initiation of combat forces training in the use of nuclear or other unconventional weapons at the tactical level;
- Serious efforts to acquire or build one or more aircraft carriers;
- Greater attention, in doctrine and training materials, to the need to acquire a true "blue water" naval capability;

- The development of a proven capacity to conduct ballistic missile attacks against ships maneuvering at sea; and
- The development of a proven ability to disable U.S. space assets.

It is highly unlikely that Hu Jintao, the new Chinese Communist Party general secretary and the president of China, and other new leaders will challenge the general direction of Chinese security strategy in the next three to five years. However, the Task Force believes it is important to monitor how this new generation of leaders might try to ensure the support of the PLA in a future crisis and, conversely, how the PLA endeavors to maintain political support—and resources—for continued military modernization. Tensions are possible between civilian leaders worried about pressing social needs and continuing economic reforms and a military frustrated that it may again be asked to defer making China a first-class regional power. Signs of this tension may be reflected in the PLA's share of the national budget, in the tone of the media's PLA coverage and critiques of military spending, and in indirect, yet clearly identifiable, criticism of party activities and policies by senior PLA officers or authoritative PLA journals.

Recommendation 3: Military-to-military dialogue should be broader and designed to achieve specific goals.

One of the central goals of military-to-military exchanges between the United States and China should be to increase Chinese defense transparency. Frank discussions between military organizations may not lower the level of suspicion among officers at the senior and lower levels of both the U.S. and Chinese militaries. Such dialogue, however, may reduce mutual misperceptions of intentions that could result in unintended conflict.

The United States should try to engage China in detailed discussions of Chinese doctrine and military planning, make thorough assessments of regional and global security issues, and hold discussions about the purpose and progress of PLA force restructuring and modernization. Specific departments of the PLA that should be engaged in these discussions include the General Staff Department Operations (Sub)Department, the General Armaments Department, the Second Artillery (the name for China's missile force) Command, the Academy of Military Sciences, and the military region headquarters. The United States should try to gain access to a wide range of ground, air, naval, nuclear, and command installations across China.

In addition to continuing more routine military-to-military exchanges, the Task Force recommends that the U.S. government identify and initiate exchanges with influential published PLA authors. Many of the analysts who regularly interpret U.S. intentions and power in PLA newspapers and journals have never been to the United States or met an American military officer. Discussion between these authors and their American counterparts, based on their published writings, would be useful in reducing misperception and miscalculation on both sides.

The Task Force also takes particular note of the importance of utilizing openly published Chinese language materials on the PLA and its modernization, and calls for increased U.S. government support for efforts to collect, translate, and analyze PLA materials. From these materials, a number of analytical questions should be pursued: Among PLA sources, what are the more and less authoritative materials? What debates exist within the PLA and how meaningful are they? How different are PLA from non-PLA views on strategic issues? And who in the civil bureaucracy, think tanks, and society in general are likely to make arguments counter to some of the PLA's preferences and interests?

Recommendation 4: Initiate semigovernmental talks on crisis management issues.

Past acrimonious encounters between the United States and China over such issues as the accidental bombing of the Chinese embassy in Belgrade, Serbia, in 1999 and the collision of U.S. and PRC military aircraft near Hainan Island in 2001, as well as the possibility of even more serious encounters in the future over Taiwan, clearly suggest the need for both countries to improve the manner in which they anticipate or address potential or actual political-military crises. The United States and China should support the initiation of extended semigovernmental discussions designed to achieve such objectives. In this context, semigovernmental dialogue means talks between former officials, strategists, and scholars on both sides with the knowledge and support of their respective governments, but no action on behalf of their respective governments. Such talks would be relatively informal and unofficial, but with links to each government.

Recommendation 5: Enter into strategic dialogue with China over missile defense and nuclear modernization.

Over the coming years, China and the United States will need to wrestle with evolving perceptions (and misperceptions) of one another's strategic doctrinal shifts. The Task Force judges, in accordance with published CIA estimates, that China has straightforward means available to overcome the U.S. national missile defense now planned for deployment and that China will do what is required to maintain and strengthen its own nuclear deterrent. Washington should state clearly and consistently to Beijing that U.S. missile defense plans are not aimed at China and that they neither signal hostile long-term intentions on the part of the United States toward China nor are they intended to negate a minimal Chinese deterrent.

The Task Force commends President George W. Bush's personal call to President Jiang Zemin to notify him of the U.S. intention to withdraw from the Anti-Ballistic Missile (ABM) Treaty and to express interest in holding strategic stability talks. But the Task Force believes more follow-up is necessary. The United States and China should hold separate discussions on issues relating to nuclear strategic stability. Chinese interlocutors should include persons from the Second Artillery, the General Staff Department, the General Armaments Department, and the Academy of Military Sciences.

The agenda for these discussions should include each side's nuclear modernization plans and nuclear doctrine, the basis of strategic stability in an environment that includes both offensive and defensive weapons, space warfare issues, and U.S. and Chinese missile defense programs. More specific questions that should be pursued include: How can China corroborate its NFU doctrine on nuclear weapons, and what does the PLA think about nuclear signaling?

Recommendation 6: Call for greater transparency in the PLA budget process.

Beijing's decision in the late 1990s to begin issuing Defense White Papers is a welcome development, and the latest edition (2002) shows modest progress in providing the most basic information about the PLA and the Chinese defense establishment. The Task Force suggests, however, that China could do much more by adhering to internationally recognized templates of defense spending (such as those of the Association of Southeast Asian Nations [ASEAN] Regional Forum, the UN Arms Register, NATO, the World Bank, the International Monetary Fund [IMF], the Stockholm International Peace Research Institute, or the International Institute for Strategic Studies).

As mentioned above, U.S. government agencies' estimates of the size of the PLA budget vary widely. How estimates of Chinese military expenditures are arrived at is as important to the U.S. understanding of Chinese military trends as are the estimates themselves. The CIA estimates the size of the budget at somewhere between $45 billion and $65 billion. Department of Defense estimates range from $65 billion to $80 billion. Neither of these estimates has been broken down, nor have the respective reports explicated their methodologies.

The Task Force believes that the U.S. government should mount a more disciplined effort to arrive at an estimate of various categories of the Chinese military budget and to acquire a more accurate picture of the Chinese military resource allocation process, with regards to both the PLA and the entire military budget. Unless a consensus can be reached as to what comprises the PLA budget, the "battle of estimates" loses much of its explanatory value and policy relevance.

Recommendation 7: Revisit the issue.

The Task Force stresses that estimating Chinese military capabilities beyond two decades is simply not feasible. Events will change the predicted course, and the United States should be prepared to respond accordingly. In sum, our report is not the last word on the subject. Rather, the report is an effort to create benchmarks. The Task Force will continue to monitor Chinese developments and, depending on circumstances, will reconvene to reconsider Chinese capabilities and U.S. policy.

TASK FORCE REPORT

Introduction

The People's Republic of China (PRC) is currently engaged in a comprehensive military modernization. This report addresses the state of China's military capabilities, assesses the current capabilities of the People's Liberation Army (PLA), and establishes milestones for judging the evolution of Chinese military power over the next twenty years. These assessments and milestones will provide policymakers and the public with a pragmatic and nonpartisan approach to measuring the development of Chinese military power. They will allow observers of Chinese military modernization to determine the degree to which changes in the quantity and quality of China's military power may threaten the interests of the United States, its allies, and its friends, as well as how the United States should adjust and respond politically, diplomatically, economically, and militarily to China's military development.

The report issues a double warning: first, against overreaction to the large scale of China's military modernization program; and second, against underreaction based on the relative backwardness of the People's Liberation Army compared with U.S. military power. Attributing to the PLA capabilities it does not have and will not attain for many years could result in the misallocation of scarce resources. Overreaction could lead the United States to adopt policies and undertake actions that become a self-fulfilling prophecy, provoking an otherwise avoidable antagonistic relationship that will not serve long-term U.S. interests. Underreaction, on the other hand, might allow China to someday catch unawares the United States or its friends and allies in Asia.

In analyzing the likely evolution of PLA capabilities, this report not only describes development processes and institutional, technological, personnel, doctrinal, and other systemic issues internal to the Chinese military establishment; it also takes into account the economic, political, strategic, and technological context shaping modernization. This larger context motivates, structures, and, at times, constrains military modernization as much as the factors emerging from within the Chinese military.

METHODOLOGY

This report is the product of an intensive project that lasted more than a year. The Task Force convened ten times during this period, and scholars and experts provided comprehensive presentations on all the services of the PLA, information warfare, civil-military relations, China's national security environment, the PLA budget process, and Chinese defense industries, as well as on the political and military situation across the Taiwan Strait. In addition, three subgroups met separately to analyze the political, economic, and technological context of military modernization. These subgroups reported their findings to the full Task Force.

Building an analytic framework for evaluating Chinese military power is difficult. The further into the future we peer, the harder it is to predict capabilities and intentions. We can reach relatively well-informed judgments about PLA capabilities in 2008; similar judgments about 2018 are highly speculative; and comparing PRC to U.S. capabilities in 2028 is still more difficult.

These difficulties are compounded because of the relative lack of transparency in the Chinese defense establishment. The direction in which the Chinese military appears to be moving is easier to determine than the rate at which it progresses given information in the public domain. Chinese doctrinal writing, declared budget priorities, arms purchases, training innovations, and reform of personnel management systems provide a fairly good picture of the capabilities the PLA hopes to develop and the types of wars it wants to be able to fight and win. The speed at which the PLA is able to travel down this road is another, and much less certain, matter.

The Task Force is aware of the problem of "mirror imaging"— the tendency to equate a potential enemy's situation with one's own, whether strategically, organizationally, culturally, or materially. The United States must not limit its assessment of potential Chinese capabilities to traditional U.S. plans for war. The PLA may try to solve problems in a manner considered unlikely or unsatisfactory by U.S. defense planners.

The issues of Chinese military modernization have been raised before in other reports, books, articles, and conference proceedings.[1] With some notable exceptions, these studies have tended to adopt one of two approaches: a focus on the absolute increas-

---

[1] An incomplete list from just the last several years includes: Department of Defense, *2002 Annual Report on the Military Power of the People's Republic of China* (July 2002); *Report to the Congress of the U.S.-China Security Review Commission* (July 2002); National Intelligence Council, *China and Weapons of Mass Destruction: Implications for the United States* (1999); David Shambaugh, *Modernizing China's Military: Progress, Problems, and Prospects* (Berkeley, CA: University of California Press, 2003); James C. Mulvenon and Andrew N.D. Yang (ed.), *The People's Liberation Army as Organization: Reference Volume V. 1.0* (RAND, 2002); Solomon M. Karmel, *China and the People's Liberation Army* (New York, NY: St. Martin's Press, 2000); Larry M. Wortzel (ed.), *The Chinese Armed Forces in the 21st Century* (U.S. Army War College Strategic Studies Institute, 1999); Susan Puska (ed.), *The People's Liberation Army After Next* (Carlisle, PA: U.S. Army War College Strategic Studies Institute, 2000); James R. Lilley and David L. Shambaugh (ed.), *China's Military Faces the Future* (Armonk, NY: M.E. Sharpe, 1999); James C. Mulvenon and Andrew N.D. Yang (ed.), *The People's Liberation Army in the Information Age* (RAND, 1999); You Ji, *The Armed Forces of China* (London: I.B. Tauris, 1999); Michael D. Swaine, *The Role of the Chinese Military in National Security Policymaking* (RAND, 1998); Robert S. Ross, "Navigating the Taiwan Strait: Deterrence, Escalation Dominance, and U.S.-China Relations," *International Security*, Vol. 27, Issue 2 (Fall 2002); Thomas J. Christensen, "Posing Problems Without Catching Up: China's Rise and the Challenge for American Security," *International Security*, Vol. 25, Issue 4 (Spring 2001); Michael O'Hanlon, "Why China Cannot Conquer Taiwan," *International Security*, Vol. 25, Issue 1 (Summer 2000); James Lilley and Carl Ford, "China's Military: A Second Opinion," *National Interest*, No. 57 (Fall 1999); Bates Gill and Michael O'Hanlon, "China's Hollow Military," *The National Interest*, No. 56 (Summer 1999); Andrew Scobell and Larry M. Wortzel (ed.), *China's Growing Military Power: Perspectives on Security, Ballistic Missiles, and Conventional Capabilities* (Carlisle, PA: U.S. Army War College Strategic Studies Institute, 2002); *The PLA and Chinese Society in Transition: Conference Proceedings*, (Washington, D.C: National Defense University, 2001); *Fourth Annual Conference on China's People's Liberation Army: Conference Proceedings* (Staunton Hill, VA: American Enterprise Institute, August 1993).

es in the quantity and quality of weapons systems acquired by China (from abroad or domestically); or an emphasis on the organizational, technological, and economic barriers to deploying and using these weapons effectively and the continued relative backwardness of the People's Liberation Army.

Comparing the backwardness of the PLA with the U.S. military is not the most fruitful analytical approach given the distinct political and strategic concerns of the Chinese leadership. Rather, the Task Force has tried to place potential PRC military capabilities in the context of their intended uses. In the case of Taiwan, the ends to which Beijing might apply force may well involve political pressure and potentially coercive actions short of actual war fighting. PRC decisions to use force might be based on calculations other than (or in addition to) a simple assessment of the quantity and quality of U.S., Taiwanese, and PRC forces. It is also important to assess PLA capabilities relative to those of other Asian militaries, rather than to U.S. forces alone.

It is likewise difficult and risky to reach conclusions about Chinese strategic and political intentions from PLA military developments. The Task Force cautions against making a direct link between what the PLA thinks and does and what the Chinese leadership intends. We do suggest some indicators of future military capabilities to watch. These capabilities may offer insights into intentions, but the capabilities of the Chinese military cannot be automatically mapped onto the intentions of the country's leadership.

This Task Force focused on military issues. It has not addressed in detail the future evolution of Sino-American relations, which will set the context of Chinese military planning. Political factors— in China, in the United States, and in Taiwan—will determine the nature of the bilateral relationship. The political implications of China's military modernization will depend as much on the policies of the United States and China's neighbors as on the military balance itself.

CURRENT CHINESE MILITARY CAPABILITIES

Overview

The Council on Foreign Relations Independent Task Force on Chinese Military Power finds that the People's Republic of China is pursuing a deliberate and focused course of military modernization, but that China is at least two decades behind the United States in terms of military technology and capability. Moreover, if the United States continues to dedicate significant resources to improving its military forces, as expected, the balance between the United States and China, both globally and in Asia, is likely to remain decisively in America's favor beyond the next twenty years.

There are multiple drivers of China's military modernization. The PLA, along with the People's Armed Police and the People's Militia, helps maintain domestic stability and ensure regime security. China is developing limited power-projection capabilities to deal with a range of possible conflict scenarios along its periphery, especially in maritime areas. The PLA is acquiring military capabilities designed to defend Chinese sovereignty and territorial interests and to pose a credible threat to Taiwan in order to influence Taiwan's choices about its political future or, failing that, to prevent Taiwan from achieving political independence. These capabilities are also intended to deter, delay, or complicate U.S. efforts to intervene on behalf of Taiwan. In addition, military modernization is expected to enhance China's international prestige.

China is a regional power, and the Task Force does not envisage China becoming a globally committed military power in the next two decades. If current trends continue (e.g., if Japan continues to eschew a role as a major regional military power), the Task Force expects that China will become the predominant military power among the nations of East Asia. China's current force structure and doctrine provide effective "defense-in-depth" against any effort to invade and seize Chinese territory. That structure includes several million paramilitary and militia personnel. The PLA possesses power projection across land borders against smaller regional powers and the ability to dislodge those powers from nearby disputed land and maritime territories. In the next two decades, the Task Force expects China will acquire a greater capability to hold and seize such territories against combined regional forces.

However, the Task Force also notes that although China will have the enduring advantages of proximity to Asia, Beijing has traditionally been weakest and the United States has traditionally been strongest in the maritime, aerospace, and technological dimensions of military power. Consequently, although China is already the strongest continental military power in East Asia and destined to become an even greater power beyond its littoral borders, a sustained and robust U.S. naval and air presence can likely offset the ability of Beijing to leverage future military capabilities into a real advantage against U.S. and allied interests in the Asia-Pacific region over the next twenty years, if not longer.

The Taiwan Strait is an area of near-term military concern. Current Chinese policy is to avoid a military confrontation if at all possible. For the next decade, a focal point of Chinese military development will likely remain achieving the ability to influence Taiwan's choices about its political future or, failing that, to prevent Taiwan from achieving formal independence. Here, China is more likely to use new technologies and asymmetric strategies, not to invade Taiwan outright but rather to achieve political goals such as forcing the resumption of political dialogue between the two sides on the mainland's terms. In a crisis, China may also use its military to counter Taiwan's economic prosperity by blockade, laying mines in the Taiwan Strait, or other means. Moreover, Beijing could decide to utilize force against Taiwan under certain circumstances even if the balance of forces across the strait favored the United States and Taiwan.

The PLA currently has the ability to undertake intensive, short-duration air, missile, and naval attacks on Taiwan, as well as more prolonged air and naval attacks. The efficacy of either scenario would be highly dependent on Taiwan's political and military response, and especially on any actions taken by the United States and Japan.

Although U.S. forces would ultimately prevail in a military crisis or conflict, Beijing might be able to impose serious risks and costs on the U.S. military if the United States concluded that it was necessary to commit air and naval forces to battle with China in defense of Taiwan. Sovremenny-class destroyers armed with Sunburn antiship missiles and Kilo-class submarines armed with wake-homing torpedoes—plus the almost two dozen older submarines China could put to sea—could slow the intervention of a naval task force.

Any conflict across the Taiwan Strait would have an extremely adverse impact on the strategic landscape in Asia, regardless of the military outcome. Therefore, the most critical element of U.S. strategy in the cross-strait situation is to deter and minimize the chances that such a crisis will occur. Taiwan is fundamentally a political issue, and any effective strategy must coordinate military measures designed to deter with diplomatic efforts to reassure both China and Taiwan credibly that their worst fears will not materialize. For U.S. policy toward Taiwan, this means providing Taiwan with weapons and assistance deemed necessary to the creation of a robust defense capability and not making a deal with Beijing behind Taipei's back. For U.S. policy toward China, it means maintaining the clear ability and willingness to counter an application of military force against Taiwan while conveying to Beijing a credible U.S. commitment to not support Taiwan's taking unilateral steps toward de jure independence.

The Task Force expects that the United States will continue to possess overwhelming dominance over China's nuclear forces for the foreseeable future. China, however, is improving the survivability of its small, retaliatory, "countervalue" deterrent force. China's nuclear arsenal will likely expand in number and sophistication over the next ten to twenty years. Although the Task Force is uncertain about the specific impact of U.S. missile defense plans on Chinese nuclear modernization in terms of numbers and force deployment, we believe that China will do whatever it can to ensure that a U.S. missile defense system cannot negate its ability to launch and deliver a retaliatory second strike.

Development of Limited Power-Projection Capabilities
China is shifting from a continental orientation requiring large land forces for "in-depth" defense to a combined continental and maritime orientation that requires a smaller, more mobile and more technologically advanced "active peripheral defense" capability. The PLA will eventually develop a limited power-projection capability through the acquisition of new weapons platforms and innovations in doctrine and training—especially by the air, naval, and missile forces.

Air Force
With the introduction of new weapons and the improvement of pilot training, the People's Liberation Army Air Force (PLAAF) has made some progress extending its capabilities beyond air-to-air interceptions and limited air-to-ground strikes. China has acquired 100-plus fourth-generation fighters (SU-27s and SU-30s) from Russia since the early 1990s. These aircraft are far more advanced than any other fighter in the PLAAF's inventory. Used primarily for high-altitude interception, capable of Mach 2.35, and very maneuverable in high-altitude combat, the SU-27 has been compared to the American F-15C. The aircraft carries six radar-homing Alamo air-to-air missiles (AAMs) and Archer infrared AAMs. The SU-30, which has a range of 3,000 kilometers, has the air combat capabilities of the SU-27 as well as ground attack and close air support capabilities. The SU-30 has more advanced avionics and radar than the SU-27 and gives the PLAAF for the first time the capability to fly missions far from the coastline. In addition, PLAAF pilots now engage in more realistic combat training exercises.

Despite these improvements, the PLAAF still has limited capability to conduct ground and naval support, air-to-air interception, and ground attack. The PLAAF has had difficulty integrating the new fourth-generation aircraft. Pilot training, while improving, also remains a challenge. Sortie generation is a problem, and the PLAAF would have difficulty sustaining an extended air campaign. The PLAAF lacks demonstrated off-shore, long-range bomber or long-range strike aircraft capability. It also lacks an operational, in-flight refueling capacity for more than 100 aircraft (four regiments), an airborne early warning and control capability, and a strategic warning and real-time surveillance and reconnaissance capability.

The PLAAF has difficulty with joint operations (simultaneous fighting with aircraft and ground or naval forces) and probably does not have the capability to do real-time reconnaissance—its aircraft are strictly controlled by ground-based command-and-control systems. Although new surface-to-air missiles (SAMs) give China a much-improved air defense capability, the PLAAF would have little air point defense and little confidence that it could protect airfields near the coast against an adversary with stealth and long-distance strike capabilities.

Navy

The People's Liberation Army Navy (PLAN) is working to develop a new generation of surface combatants with improved air defense, antisubmarine, and antiship capabilities; modern conventional and nuclear attack submarines with advanced torpedoes and cruise missile capabilities; an improved naval air arm; and greatly improved replenishment-at-sea capabilities.

China's most advanced destroyer is the Russian Sovremenny-class destroyer. The Sovremenny, specifically designed to counter U.S. Aegis-class destroyers, is a major improvement for the PLAN. The destroyer carries Russian Sunburn antiship missiles, which are among the most advanced in the world and against which there are only limited countermeasures. The PLAN is also seeking more capable antiship cruise missiles and land-attack cruise missiles (LACMs). The Kilo-class submarine, also procured from Russia, is another impressive advance for the PLAN, especially when armed with wake-homing torpedoes.

The PLAN is limited by a lack of integration in its command, control, and communication systems; targeting; air defense; and antisubmarine warfare capabilities. PLAN ships are vulnerable to attack by aircraft, torpedoes, and antiship missiles. The navies of the ASEAN nations could, if able to operate together, exclude the PLAN from the South China Sea.

Missiles

China is improving the survivability of its small, retaliatory, "countervalue" deterrent force. This transition implies, over the medium-to-long term, the development of a larger (yet still relatively small) number of land- and sea-based longer-range ballistic missiles with improved range, accuracy, survivability, and penetration against a limited missile defense system. These missiles are likely to be fitted with smaller nuclear warheads. China also expects to develop a modern strategic surveillance, early warning, and battle management system, with advanced land, airborne, and space-based command, control, communications, computers, intelligence, surveillance, and reconnaissance (C^4ISR) assets.

In addition, some PLA analysts have argued that China should acquire a more sophisticated conventional missile capability in response to the United States' technologically superior conventional theater-oriented strike assets. This includes more mobile and accurate short-range ballistic missiles (SRBMs) as well as LACMs.

PLA MODERNIZATION IN POLITICAL CONTEXT

China's defense modernization serves both internal and external objectives, and it is influenced by both domestic and external variables. China's leaders must make trade-offs between the objectives of promoting economic development and greater integration into the world economy; maintaining political stability; and defending territorial integrity, including preventing Taiwan from moving closer to independence. Given these multiple objectives, at times Beijing may prioritize some goals over others, and it may adopt a changing mix of domestic and foreign policies in pursuit of these goals.

Domestic Goals

For the foreseeable future, China is preoccupied with domestic problems—ensuring a smooth political succession; mitigating the dangers arising from the massive burden of nonperforming loans and a potential banking crisis; curbing rising unemployment;

reforming state-owned enterprises; modernizing the legal system; ameliorating growing social and regional inequality; combating rampant official corruption; improving the environment; dealing with AIDS, SARS, and other public health crises; and dampening popular unrest. China's leaders, including those now stepping into top party and government positions, appear to have reached a strong consensus on the prime importance of a peaceful international environment in general and good relations with the United States in particular—external conditions conducive to dealing with their challenging domestic agenda. The recent leadership succession is unlikely to change strategic goals in the near term, especially with Jiang Zemin both retaining the chairmanship of the Central Military Commission and maintaining a strong influence within the civilian political leadership.

The primary domestic goals of China's leaders are maintaining the rule and survival of the Chinese Communist Party, promoting economic development, ensuring national unity, and preventing domestic unrest. The PLA is concerned with achieving its professional mission (being able to fight "limited wars under high-tech conditions"), protecting its political standing and influence, and maintaining, if not expanding, its share of national resources.

The current state of civil-military relations dates back to the mid-1990s and represents an important change from the previous two decades. For much of the 1980s and the early 1990s, there was a broad civil-military understanding that limited PLA budgets, promising eventual benefits once the rewards of economic reform were realized. During these years, China's main focus was fostering economic growth by reforming the moribund centrally planned economy. Defense was clearly the fourth of the "Four Modernizations" (agriculture, industry, science and technology, and defense). The PLA lacked funding for major equipment modernization and had to "do more with less" by professionalizing and streamlining. PLA modernization during this period was characterized mainly by troop reductions and some improvements in training and personnel management.

The terms of this understanding changed in the mid-1990s. An altered security environment and new assessments of the changing nature of warfare motivated the PLA to dedicate itself to becoming a more professional and operationally competent military. The altered security environment centered on Taiwan and a growing antagonism with the United States as well as on new U.S. capabilities. Developing a defense against the enormous U.S. capabilities for long-range precision guided munitions, stealth attack, and real-time battle management became a pressing challenge for the PLA.

In addition, rapid economic growth permitted defense budget increases and weapons purchases from abroad. Increased central government revenues allowed the civilian leadership to reward the PLA for quelling the demonstrations in Tiananmen Square, to fulfill its promise to dedicate more resources to military modernization once the larger economic reform program was underway, and to compensate the military as it withdrew from commercial ventures after 1998. Since the early 1990s, real military spending has increased.

Taiwan

The long-term primary objective of PRC leaders vis-à-vis Taiwan is to achieve reunification on Beijing's terms. China's near-term objective is to stabilize the relationship and to make tangible progress toward some sort of reunification with Taiwan or at least to prevent further movement toward independence. China's current Taiwan strategy consists of four parts: military leverage; economic integration; "united front" tactics of reaching out to Taiwanese business people and political factions within the Kuomintang, Democratic Progressive Party, and People First Party, while isolating President Chen Shui-bian; and squeezing Taiwan on the international stage. Within the strategy of military leverage, the PLA's objective has been to acquire the military capability required to demonstrate sufficient power to influence a political/diplomatic outcome on the Taiwan issue; and/or the ability to deny, delay, or deter U.S. intervention in support of Taiwan.

China currently has a preference for a peaceful resolution of the Taiwan situation and in recent years has taken a more conciliatory line. Beijing apparently believes that while political currents may be moving in a worrying direction toward greater support for Taiwanese independence, economic developments promoting interdependence across the Taiwan Strait and military trends increasing Chinese leverage are moving in Beijing's favor. Still, these trends may reverse; or Beijing may perceive them to be reversing even if they are not, and China may again in the future rely more on coercive measures.

The impulses of China's military modernization are multiple. Bureaucratic politics, interservice rivalry, industrial policy, and the reality that China has long land and sea borders to defend all motivate military modernization. Taiwan provides the mission around which the PLA can organize some aspects of modernization, but, like their counterparts in the United States, Chinese defense planners are grappling with threat-based (Taiwan) versus capabilities-based (uncertain futures with the United States, Russia, India, and Japan, and on the Korean Peninsula) scenarios.

External Goals
The primary external goals of China's leaders are the achievement of China's hoped-for place of respect and influence within the established institutions of the international system; the defense of territorial integrity; the completion of China's full integration into the global economy; and the promotion of a peaceful regional and international environment supportive of domestic economic growth.

Within this framework, PLA modernization addresses specific military and political objectives: the securing of Beijing's interests along the periphery of China's eastern and southeastern provinces; the eventual acquisition of power-projection and extended territorial-defense capabilities commensurate with regional power status; and the enhancement of China's international prestige. Although China is increasingly a great power economically and diplomatically—the resolution of a wide range of international issues increasingly requires the participation of China—great power status as a military power lies beyond China's present capabilities.

This study has occurred during a time of rapid change. The world looks very different after the terrorist attacks of September 11, 2001. Beijing's assessments of the overall strategic environment and of China's place in the world immediately after September 11 are probably mixed. Events that are likely to worry Beijing include the victory in Iraq, NATO's continued expansion, the war in Afghanistan and the stationing of U.S. troops in Central Asia, U.S. military cooperation with India, and the U.S. withdrawal from the Anti-Ballistic Missile (ABM) Treaty.

There are other longer-term trends that may balance Beijing's negative assessment of China's place in the world. Most important, Chinese officials apparently believe that time is on China's side. In Beijing's view, China's leverage—economic, diplomatic, and military—continues to grow relative to the United States and all other actors.

United States

Sino-American relations have significantly improved since the EP-3 incident, when a Chinese fighter plane collided with a U.S. Navy surveillance aircraft, in April 2001. Putting aside the most volatile issues in the bilateral relationship, both sides have found new areas of cooperation, in particular the war against terrorism, nonproliferation, and the management of tensions on the Korean Peninsula. Beijing has benefited from a shift in U.S. strategic priorities—away from worry about the rise of a potential "peer competitor" to concerns about terrorism and weapons of mass destruction—as well as from Washington's need to avoid problems with China as it addresses crises in Iraq and North Korea. Beijing also now recognizes that a more confrontational approach to foreign policy and denunciations of alleged American "hegemonism" are only likely to provoke a hostile response in Washington.

How long Sino-American cooperation lasts will depend in part on relations across the Taiwan Strait. Over the next five to ten years, a Taiwan scenario remains the only real possibility for major armed conflict between the United States and China. Both the

PLA and the U.S. military increasingly view each other through the prism of a such a scenario. Much of Beijing's current confidence about Sino-American relations rests on positive perceptions of the state of cross-strait relations and the U.S.-China-Taiwan triangle. This confidence could be severely dented by increased U.S. military cooperation with Taiwan or the perception that the United States is supporting a move toward Taiwanese independence.

Any conflict across the Taiwan Strait would, and even a crisis short of conflict could, have an extremely adverse impact on the strategic landscape in Asia, regardless of the military outcome. Therefore, the most critical element of U.S. strategy in the cross-strait situation is to minimize the chances that such a crisis will occur. Taiwan is fundamentally a political issue, and any effective strategy must coordinate military measures designed to deter with diplomatic efforts to reassure both China and Taiwan credibly that their worst fears will not materialize. For U.S. policy toward Taiwan, this means providing Taiwan with weapons and assistance deemed necessary to the creation of a robust defense capability while not making a deal with Beijing behind Taipei's back. For U.S. policy toward China, it means maintaining the clear ability and willingness to counter any application of military force against Taiwan while conveying to Beijing a credible U.S. commitment to not support Taiwan's taking unilateral steps toward de jure independence.

Russia

Among China's other external relations, its relationship with Russia is the one most likely to influence the pace and scope of PRC military modernization. China is critically dependent on Russia for more advanced weapons and defense technologies as well as spare parts and repairs. Suspicion by either side of the other's strategic intentions could derail the relationship. Since this supply relationship is a significant vulnerability for the Chinese, China would like to reduce its dependence on Russia, although the poor state of China's own defense industries remains a significant impediment to achieving this goal.

Japan

Sino-Japanese relations are characterized both by deep historical suspicions and by political and economic cooperation, as well as by growing security concerns. There are a number of issues that affect the tone of the security relationship and long-term defense planning in both countries, such as Chinese missile development and the expansion of Japan's Maritime Self-Defense Force.

Some Chinese leaders are increasingly wary of the goals of the U.S.-Japan alliance. This suspicion emerges from a belief that the alliance was strengthened in order to facilitate U.S.-Japanese cooperation in defense of Taiwan and more broadly to contain or constrain China's ability to exert greater influence in the region. The 2002 China Defense White Paper expressed concerns over joint U.S.-Japan research on a missile defense system. Some Chinese analysts have also expressed reservations about the dispatch of a Japanese destroyer armed with the Aegis system to protect replenishment ships in support of U.S. troops in Afghanistan. These concerns are part of larger Chinese fears that Japan may consider a constitutional revision and eventual remilitarization.

In November 2002, a task force sponsored by Prime Minister Junichiro Koizumi of Japan released a report designating China as Japan's top foreign policy priority for the immediate future. Citing concerns that China's military buildup could pose a serious threat to Japan, the report called for greater transparency in China's military modernization. Japanese defense analysts are closely monitoring the development of short-range missiles and anticarrier and other antiship capabilities by China.

Korea

Korea is the key area of change since the Task Force began its work in February 2002. Beijing is seriously concerned about the prospect of a nuclear North Korea (the Democratic People's Republic of Korea, or DPRK). The potential proliferation consequences of a nuclear North Korea—with South Korea and Japan possibly developing their own nuclear capabilities in response—threaten China's security interests. In addition, a resumption of North Korean ballistic missile tests could destabilize the region and provide further justification for a U.S. deployment of theater missile defenses.

Despite Beijing's opposition to a nuclear Korean Peninsula, preventing or rolling back a North Korean nuclear program is only one of China's objectives. Beijing wants to avoid the implosion of the DPRK since such a collapse would have massive human and economic consequences for China. Given these considerations, Beijing is unlikely to support economic sanctions or a military strike against the DPRK. China's preferred strategy in the current crisis is a multilateral deal that trades North Korea's abandonment of weapons of mass destruction for the normalization of relations between North Korea and the United States and that encourages broad economic reforms in North Korea.

India

China and India increasingly compete for political and economic influence in the region. Indian policymakers and defense analysts are concerned about future power projection by China and have expressed repeated unease about Chinese activities in Burma, particularly those with relevance to the Andaman Sea and the Indian Ocean. Chinese analysts are monitoring increased coordination between the U.S. and Indian militaries. Both India and China pay careful attention to developments in the other's military, especially in the areas of missiles, nuclear weapons, fourth-generation aircraft, and "blue water" navy capabilities.

Other Regions

As long as the arms and defense technology embargo levied by the United States and Europe after 1989 remains in place, Europe's importance to China will continue to be mainly political and commercial in nature, while the South China Sea and Central Asia will continue to be areas of significant concern for Chinese leaders. Major developments in those areas could affect deployments but are less likely to affect the overall military modernization program than are factors relating to Taiwan, the United States, Japan, India, Korea, and Russia.

International Organizations

During the 1990s, Beijing increasingly moved in the direction of integration with the established global and multilateral systems, including trade agreements, treaties, and UN activities. The decision to sign the Comprehensive Test Ban Treaty, for example, reflected Beijing's conclusion that China could not be seen to be outside of what was considered a globally accepted treaty and judgment of the satisfactory state of China's nuclear weapons development. In addition, China's hosting of the 2008 Olympics creates an even greater need to avoid additional external tensions.

Given current domestic and international challenges, Beijing requires a secure external environment, centered on stable U.S.-China ties, so that it can concentrate on domestic challenges. The PLA will continue to develop limited power-projection capabilities over the next five years. Current Chinese priorities, however, offer the potential for the United States to influence through diplomatic, political, and military measures both longer-term Chinese plans for military modernization and Beijing's policies relating to the threat of the use of force.

PLA REFORMS AND DEVELOPMENT ASPIRATIONS

PLA force deployments are basically unchanged since the mid-1970s and 1980s: ground forces remain concentrated in north China; the air force, though more broadly based than either the navy or army, is tied to the army's military regions and retains a significant concentration of bases near Taiwan in the Nanjing and Guangzhou military regions; and the navy is distributed among the North, East, and South Sea Fleets. The most notable change in force deployment was the expansion of the PLA's short-range ballistic missile forces during the late 1990s and the deployment of almost 400 SRBMs across from Taiwan.

The elements of PLA modernization fit loosely into three categories: (1) the development, procurement, acquisition, and fielding of new weapon technologies; (2) the development of new operational concepts and joint war-fighting doctrines for weapons deployment and "employment" (i.e., the use of these new weapons); and (3) an array of institutional reforms necessary to underwrite the first two categories.

In the next two sections, the Task Force notes important changes in doctrine and progress in personnel reform. The acquisition of specific weapons platforms and recent improvements in training are discussed in more detail in the following sections dealing with the needs of the specific services—ground, air, naval, missile, and information warfare forces. These sections include discussions of development programs and future aspirations as well as of factors that continue to trouble these programs and could slow the PLA's attainment of its goals.

The Task Force has tried to demarcate clearly the differences among three conceptual categories: current capabilities, development programs, and future aspirations. By "capabilities" the Task Force means both the military hardware currently possessed by the PLA and the ability of the Chinese military to train with, deploy, logistically support, and employ these weapons. The Task Force has also linked capabilities to specific military, political, and strategic goals. We use "development programs" to designate those capabilities the PLA is currently developing but has not yet mastered. China is likely to develop many of these capabilities over the next ten to fifteen years. "Aspirations" suggests those programs the Chinese military is most likely to try to develop in the future given strategic intentions and military needs but which the Chinese military may not master over the next two decades or longer.

Doctrinal Innovation
Compared with the U.S. military, doctrine in the Chinese military tends to be less operational and practical and more of a construct, guiding the development of PLA capabilities and posture. Still, analyzing Chinese writings provides a sense of baseline aspirations.

Since the early 1990s, the need to create a PLA able to fight and win "limited wars under high-tech conditions" has been the guiding principle of Chinese military modernization. "Limited wars under high-tech conditions" are conflicts with limited political objectives and geographic scope and short in duration but with decisive strategic outcomes. They are usually fought over territorial claims, economic disputes, or ethnic rivalries. These wars are not regionwide, much less global conflicts, but they can be very large in scale and intensity.

In such limited conflicts, a single campaign may decide an entire war. These conflicts consist of high-intensity operations, based on mobility, speed, and deep reach; they employ high-technology weapons that produce high lethality rates. Fought in all the battle space dimensions simultaneously (air, land, sea, electromagnetic spectrum, and outer space), these wars are information intensive and critically dependent on C^{4}ISR. They are also characterized by joint-service operations; they will produce high resource-consumption rates and thus will be critically dependent on high-speed logistics.

The PLA believes that the initial campaign in a "limited war under high-tech conditions" will likely be the decisive campaign. Once a state of hostility exists, the PLA's operational-level guidance calls for the unrelenting prosecution of offensive operations. The objective of the campaign might be to defend against an attack, but the military action is offensive. This represents a major doctrinal change for the PLA, which has typically fought wars of attrition.

In the conduct of these wars, the PLA operational-level guidance calls for adherence to the principles of "integrated operations and key-point strikes." These are multiphase operations that coordinate mobile warfare, information warfare, psychological warfare, and special operations. They are part of a larger campaign of paralysis, in which the PLA destroys an enemy's command-and-control system; cripples its campaign, information, and logistical systems; and eliminates its enemy's most advanced weapons systems.

Personnel

Over the past several years, the PLA has substantially reduced its size, and its personnel system has undergone major reforms. Downsizing the army, deactivating some units with outdated equipment and shifting some to the People's Armed Police, restructuring the naval and air units, and dismantling and merging internal organs of units at and above the corps level reduced the total size of the PLA to 2.35 million people by the end of 2001. The PLA moved in 1998 from a three-year conscription system for the army and a four-year conscription system for the air force and navy to a two-year conscription system for all the services. From 1997 to 2000, the size of the army was cut by 18.6 percent, the navy by 11.4 percent, the air force by 12.6 percent, and the Second Artillery by 2.9 percent.

Important innovations in the personnel system are occurring in several key areas: the introduction of officer accession, the development of a professional corps of noncommissioned officers (NCOs), the improvement of the officer personnel management system, and the intensification of professional military education. The PLA recognizes that in order to develop officers capable of successfully conducting limited wars under high-tech conditions, it must be able to select candidates knowledgeable in a variety of areas including advanced technologies and engineering. In an effort to meet this need, the PLA is developing widespread officer recruitment programs at civilian universities and creating a national defense scholarship program to recruit potential officers before they begin their college studies. The PLA has also expended great effort to create a corps of professional NCOs who are technically and professionally competent.

In order to improve the quality of those commanding officers already in the PLA, new regulations have increased mandatory pre-command training. The PLA also has begun to close many redundant academies in the military regions, to consolidate many of the higher quality academies, and to increase cooperation between civilian universities and military academies so as to enrich the curricula and teaching staffs.

Many of these programs have only been in effect for a few years, some for only one or two. At the end of this process, the PLA hopes to have a substantial pool of educated and experienced senior field-grade officers and junior flag officers able to deal with the sophisticated concepts involved in making the PLA a more competent world-class force. The same is hoped for in the case of junior officers and NCOs.

PLA training has since the late 1990s emphasized small-scale, specialized maneuvers consistent with the organizational and doctrinal shifts of fighting a limited war under high-tech conditions. The PLA has oriented much of its training for defense against the use of stealth aircraft, cruise missiles, and electronic warfare by a technologically advanced adversary. The People's Liberation Army Navy has exercised longer sea patrols, trained around the eastern cost of Taiwan and near the Philippines, and practiced several operations never before performed by the PLAN (e.g., airborne supply, antiship missile attacks, fire damage control, and open ocean operations). There have also been numerous reports of amphibious landing drills and other exercises seemingly in preparation for a Taiwan contingency.

PLA Ground Forces

PLA modernization efforts focus on developing units able to conduct limited, joint operation campaigns at and beyond China's borders. Reforms have created smaller, more flexible ground forces, all better motivated, trained, and equipped. These forces will be centered in rapid-reaction units possessing limited, yet increasing, airborne-drop and amphibious power-projection capabilities.

The number of ground troops has been steadily decreasing; they number 1.6 million today. Downsizing and restructuring are designed to create a standardized combined-arms force that has more modern weapons and equipment, greater mobility and firepower, and, most important, a higher state of readiness. All infantry divisions within the PLA now have armor. (Prior to 1997, only half the infantry divisions had tanks or armor assigned to them.) Also, all armored units now have mechanized infantry. Within a decade, one-third of the PLA's ground forces will be organized and equipped to conduct fully integrated combined-arms operations.

The PLA is divided into two types of ground forces, each designed for different types of missions. First, "high-priority units"—the smaller and more mobile joint-operation units—will be equipped with more technologically advanced weapons. These units, critical to the rapid projection of PLA power, will create a combined-arms army able to mobilize not only infantry formations but also combinations of infantry, armor, artillery, and combat engineers. The second type of unit is focused primarily on border defense and internal stability; these units are larger and armed with older equipment.

PLA ground forces are primarily armed with equipment from the 1950s, 1960s, and 1970s. Chinese defense industries still suffer from serious shortcomings in research and development (R&D) as well as manufacturing technology, and overseas arms purchases primarily supply the air force, navy, and the Second Artillery. One major improvement in ground force equipment worth noting is the fielding of the T-98 tank. Although made vulnerable by its heavy weight, the T-98 tank, which is the equivalent of the Russian T-72, has a powerful 125 millimeter gun and is equipped with an array of fire-control and targeting systems that make it just a half-step behind the best tanks in the West. The actual numbers of this new tank, however, appear to be small—perhaps as few as 60.

The PLA hopes to broaden the education of its leaders by providing them with a wider array of experiences and ensuring that every officer has a college degree by 2005. According to the PLA, today 80 percent of the officer corps have a college education. These degrees do not necessarily come from four-year civilian universities; many are from two-year associate college programs affiliated with military academies. Although the education level of officers is low by Western standards, these rates are an improvement for the PLA.

In addition, an on-campus officer-recruiting program is slowly being implemented at select civilian universities (often erroneously described as a reserve officer training corps [ROTC] program). A system for the creation of enhanced professional NCO corps has grown very rapidly since the implementation of the 1999 Military Service Law. Most of the NCOs are in their first three-year term, and so the end results of this process remain to be seen.

PLA training exercises have improved significantly over the last decade. Training has shifted to what the United States refers to as standards-based training, and many exercises now include the use of an opposing force. Also, some PLA training is conducted in combined-arms training centers that resemble U.S. Army training centers. There has also been significantly more joint training between the PLA ground forces and the air force and between the air force and the navy over the last five years, although still far less of each than in the United States. PLA leaders have made strides in developing an objectives-based and objectives-assessed training doctrine. In this regard, failure in training is tolerated if the problems are correctly identified and effectively addressed.

PLA Ground Forces: Continuing Issues
Developing an expeditionary (over-the-water) capability for PLA ground forces will require much greater improvements in striking depth, logistics, material, and army aviation (helicopters). Coordinating reforms across multiple areas simultaneously—doctrine, personnel, equipment, and training—has not been an easy task for the ground forces and is likely to affect both the speed of reform and its efficacy. The army's ability to manage these reforms is made even more difficult by the service's low priority compared with air, naval, and Second Artillery forces in the increasing competition for financial resources.

The cumbersome task of preparing for dual missions—power projection and the ability to reestablish domestic stability in case the People's Armed Police should fail to control disturbances—slows the pace of developing a more effective expeditionary force. In terms of actually completing these missions, PLA ground troops suffer from significant shortcomings in command-and-control, air defense, logistics, and communications.

Command-and-control will be one of the most difficult obstacles to overcome, not only because of limited equipment but also because of the overcentralization of leadership authority. Due to such shortcomings, many PLA officers resist further reducing and redeploying China's large ground force units. Such units are placed along China's periphery near where they could be expected to fight. Also, a further reduction in ground forces through demobilization presents all sorts of economic problems.

Special operations and coordination with follow-on conventional forces currently receive special attention and funding, but many problems remain to be solved. A lack of suitable, secure, and jam-resistant communications equipment, problems with rapidly transmitting data from dispersed special force units to the appropriate conventional force headquarters, and the challenges inherent in airborne and seaborne expeditionary forces maintaining continuous contact with special operations units pose daunting challenges to PLA command structures.

PLA training, although improving, contains some vestiges of Mao-era culture; many large-scale exercises are choreographed for senior leaders. Moreover, the military educational system is still more or less staffed as it was when it was created for a force of four million. Consequently, there are stagnant faculties with no operational experience, outdated curricula, and poor teaching methods.

PLA Navy

Although historically a continental/littoral force, over the next several decades the PLA Navy seeks to develop a more robust maritime capability. In the mid-1980s, the PLAN abandoned its "coastal defense" strategy and adopted an "offshore defense" one. In Chinese articulations of this strategy, "offshore" is variously defined as 150–600 nautical miles. Regardless of the specific distance, the PLAN hopes to exert greater influence over the Yellow Sea facing Japan and Korea; the western sections of the East China Sea, which include Taiwan; and the South China Sea.

For future deployments, the PLAN has been training for phased and joint operations; it seeks to develop improved command-and-control capabilities and a truly integrated computer system. The PLAN has also been further integrating certain aspects of its operations with the civilian sector, including the development of a joint PLAN and nominally civilian fuel system and the possible use of merchant ships for amphibious purposes.

In total, China has 69 submarines, 62 surface combatants, 56 amphibious ships, 39 mine warfare ships, 368 coastal patrol craft, and 3 replenishment-at-sea oilers. The operational missions for the

PLAN include attacking enemy warships, antisubmarine warfare, amphibious warfare, coastal defense, surveillance, mine warfare, merchant ship convoy, sea-air rescue, and logistics.

Given its desire to develop greater power-projection capabilities, the age of its current fleet, and the significant weaknesses of indigenously produced surface ships and submarines, the PLAN has actively tried to acquire new weapons and systems from, or develop in cooperation with, foreign suppliers, especially Russia. The most significant purchases include:

- *Nuclear-powered ballistic missile submarines:* The PLAN currently has one Xia-type, which stays in port, but it is currently developing at least one and probably more Type-094 submarines with Russian assistance.

- *Nuclear-powered attack submarines:* The PLAN has five Soviet-modeled Han-type submarines but has been only marginally successful in operating them. A new Type-093 submarine is currently under production with Russian assistance and is expected to be in use by 2005.

- *Conventionally powered attack submarines:* The PLAN added four Kilo submarines purchased from the Russians in 1995 to three Song-class subs made domestically and a few dozen older submarines, including Ming-class subs. The PLAN is maintaining a moderate production rate of the Song- and Ming-class submarines, and eight more Kilo-class vessels are on order.

- *Surface ships:* The PLAN's fleet of surface ships is currently being modernized with the purchase of Sovremenny-class destroyers. China took possession of two Sovremenny-class destroyers in 2000 and is expected to receive two more in 2006. The Sovremennys are equipped with antiship Sunburn missiles. The missile can reach targets within 130 kilometers, and the PLAN may soon acquire the follow-up to the Sunburn, the Yakhont, which possesses a longer range. China also indigenously produced one new Luhai-class destroyer.

In addition to these acquisitions, some of the biggest advances in the PLAN's modernization have been in training. The navy's

230,000 personnel now undergo advanced technical training before being stationed on a ship. A greater number of officers are college educated and groomed in nascent ROTC-type development programs. For enlisted personnel, the PLAN is now looking for at least senior middle-school graduates. There is also a petty officer corps under development. In an attempt to improve the overall efficiency of its officers and enlisted personnel, the PLAN has revamped its training academies.

The PLAN training model includes interservice training, in which surface-ship commanders are assigned to an army unit, and army unit commanders are assigned to a surface ship for up to six months. Joint training is discussed extensively in PLAN writings but has yet to develop into sophisticated exercises.

The number of aircraft in the People's Liberation Army Navy–Air Force (PLANAF) decreased markedly during the 1990s. In 1992, there were about 800; now the PLAN maintains 485 shore-based aircraft and a few dozen shipboard helicopters. Also, as in the air force, the PLAN flies primarily older aircraft. The PLAN has yet to be issued SU-27s or SU-30s.

Some of the most useful aircraft under the command of the PLANAF are the eight KA-28s (destroyer-based antisubmarine warfare helicopters) recently acquired from Russia in conjunction with the Sovremenny guided-missile-class destroyers. With the development of the appropriate C^{4}ISR, these helicopters will provide over-the-horizon targeting.

PLAN: Continuing Issues
The PLAN accounts for approximately one-third of total PLA expenses but makes up only 11 percent of total manpower. Despite these allocations, resource constraints are especially acute for the PLAN given the increasing costs of China's maritime security concerns, which include the Taiwan scenario and other sovereignty issues as well as the protection of sea lines of communication and trade in waters at least 100 nautical miles from the coast. The high cost of "big ticket" items like the Sovremenny-class destroyers (approximately $1.4 billion) and the Kilo-class submarines ($200 million) increases the financial pressure on the PLAN's budget.

History weighs heavily on the navy. Soviet doctrinal influence may still be strong and is reflected in the centralized control and secondary status of naval forces. PLAN leadership, with a few exceptions, is excluded from senior leadership positions in the PLA.

New capabilities are limited by the lack of some critical supporting systems. The PLAN is deficient in antisubmarine warfare capabilities. PLAN ships are also vulnerable to air attack by both aircraft and antiship missiles. PLAN anti-aircraft forces include the Crotale system from France and the SA-N-7 from Russia, both of which are "point defense" systems that can only lock on targets coming straight toward the launcher. The range of these missiles is also limited—about seventeen kilometers. The PLAN may soon acquire the SA-N-17 Grizzly, which possesses a 40–kilometer range, but again the fire-control system is limited.

PLA Air Force

In the past, the mission of the People's Liberation Army Air Force was primarily limited to defending China's borders against invasion, largely by air-to-air interception and, to a lesser extent, air-to-ground strike. This mission required little mobility or integration with other services. The role of the PLAAF was to support border defense as an adjunct to the missions of the ground forces.

PLAAF leaders are now seeking to build a more versatile and modern air force, with longer-range interceptor/strike aircraft, improved electronic warfare and air defense, extended and close air support, and longer-range transport, lift, and midair refueling; a joint-service, tactical-operations doctrine utilizing more sophisticated C⁴ISR, early warning, and battle management systems; and both airborne- and satellite-based assets, to improve detection, tracking, targeting, and strike capabilities and to enhance operational coordination among the armed services.

Because it does not operate independent missions, the PLAAF does not have a strategic equivalent to the PLA Navy's "offshore defense" strategy. Strategic guidelines are a PLAAF goal, but they have not yet been developed. The PLAAF focuses mainly at the campaign level of war. PLAAF writings on operations theory describe three types of air campaigns: offensive, defensive, and blockade (with blockade referring strictly to a Taiwan scenario). The same writings detail two operational modes: positional and mobile. In the past, the PLAAF has only proved capable of operating defensive positional campaigns. It is, however, working toward employing offensive mobile campaigns.

The PLAAF has the goal of operating joint-force campaigns and of using each of its branches in combined-arms operations. Currently, each of the PLAAF's five branches—aviation, surface-to-air missile units, anti-aircraft artillery, radar, and airborne forces—operates individually. The PLAAF makes clear in its writings that it sees a distinction between the role of air defense—SAMs, anti-aircraft artillery, and radar troops—and the role of aviation.

The PLAAF is markedly reducing the number of aircraft under its control. After reaching a total of 5,000 aircraft at the end of the 1980s, the PLAAF now fields only 3,500 planes—2,000 of which are the J-6s, the last of which was made in 1979. The total number of aircraft will decrease further to about 2,000 by the end of this decade, with the J-6 almost entirely eliminated. In addition, personnel reductions have continued since the late 1980s—the air force has gone from 470,000 at the end of the 1980s down to about 420,000 currently. By the end of the decade, the PLAAF will number about 300,000–320,000 personnel.

The PLAAF is modernizing its overall force structure. This includes the modification of older platforms like the J-7 and J-8 aircraft and the introduction of new weapons and airplanes. These include J-10, SU-30, SU-27/J-11, IL-76 aircraft; the H-6 tanker; airborne early warning and control systems; electronic countermeasures; special purpose aircraft; and SA-10, SA-20, AAMs, and cruise missiles. China received the first regiment of SU-27s in 1992, the first SU-27 trainers in 2000, and the first SU-30s in 2000. PLAAF pilots flew the first SU-27s assembled in Shenyang (dubbed J-11s) in 1998. The SU-27, SU-30, and J-11 are currently deployed in six military regions: Beijing, Nanjing, Guangzhou, Jinan, Shenyang, and Chengdu. For now, the PLAAF has stationed the SU-27s considerably inland, where they still have the range to reach Taiwan, or where they can stage missions from bases closer to the coast. The PLAAF is gradually integrating its SU-27s and SA-10/20 SAMs into the rest of the force.

In addition to multirole strike aircraft and air defense systems, the PLA has placed a high priority on the research, development, and production of LACMs as a key component of a PLAAF air campaign. The PLAAF is expected to field its first stand-off land-attack weapon within the next two or three years.

China currently has only one type of aircraft capable of being refueled in the air—the J-8D. Both the PLAAF and naval aviation have this airplane, as well as the H-6 aerial refueling aircraft, and naval aviation is actually doing more refueling training than the air force, although how much training is actually taking place is unknown. The PLAAF J-8Ds are stationed next to Guangzhou, and naval aviation's J-8Ds are located on Hainan Island.

The PLAAF has established airborne and fighter rapid-reaction units. The 15th Airborne Army's designation has been elevated to branch status, and its brigades have been upgraded to divisions. The 15th Airborne Army received the first Russian IL-76 transport aircraft and has successfully practiced its first landing on an island. These aircraft may provide airlift capabilities for approximately 5,000–7,000 airborne troops.

The PLAAF is gradually improving its training. It has expanded test and training centers, created "blue army" aggressor units, trained in delineated military regions, conducted joint-service training, supplemented training with the use of simulators, expanded over-water training (which was not done until the late 1990s), emphasized multiple aircraft training, and practiced in-flight refueling. The PLAAF is beginning to fly entire regiments—twenty to twenty-four aircraft—during its exercises, as opposed to just two or three planes in a squadron as it has done in the past. To realize mobile offensive warfare, the PLAAF is practicing moving and supporting regiments of a particular type of plane more often and for longer periods of time to bases outside their military regions.

PLAAF: Continuing Issues

The PLAAF leadership is inexperienced in command. In 1989, almost every senior commander was a Korean War veteran. By 1995, this group had retired and been replaced by officers with no combat experience. In addition, the PLAAF lacks commanders capable of controlling more than their own base's aircraft. Because pilots are educated in different schools and are not co-located, PLAAF commanders are trained in only one aircraft, which makes managing groups of aircraft more difficult.

Pilot training, although improving, remains an issue. The best pilots train for roughly 130 hours a year compared with the 225 hours average training time of U.S. Air Force pilots and approximately 180 hours for pilots from Taiwan. Restricted training time and lack of training specialization limits the ability of Chinese pilots to master fully a particular operation.

China's aerospace industry has consistently failed to provide many of the aircraft requested by the PLAAF. China's reliance on foreign suppliers—Russia, Israel, Italy, and France—is symptomatic of weaknesses in indigenous R&D, manufacturing, maintenance, and repair. The logistics and maintenance of the SU-27 is a good example of this problem. Although some of the planes are assembled in China, only about 10 percent of current production is of domestic content; airframes, engines, and avionics are produced in Russia.

The PLAAF must also consider flight time on the SU-27 airframes, so as to postpone sending them back to Russia for repair. Because the first fifty SU-27s were received close to ten years ago, each accruing 1,500 hours of flying time since its purchase, some aircraft will need to be returned to Russia for overhauling. When returned for maintenance, each plane will be out of the PLAAF forces for eight to twelve months. Even the J-7s and J-8s, which house Chinese-designed engines and are currently being modified by the PLAAF, rely on Russian avionics.

Second Artillery: Nuclear and Conventional Missile Forces

Nuclear Forces
In the strategic intercontinental realm, China is improving the survivability of its small, retaliatory "countervalue" deterrent force. The best estimates based on a range of official and open sources place China's current nuclear weapons arsenal at about 410–440 weapons. These weapons fall roughly into three categories. About 140 are warheads deployed with China's medium- and long-range land- and sea-based missile forces. About the same number (approximately 150) are designated for use with China's nuclear-capable aircraft. Another third of China's nuclear weapons (about 120–150) may be for low-yield tactical bombardment, artillery shells, atomic demolition munitions, and possibly short-range missiles such as the DF-15 and DF-11. These figures are highly uncertain; some Chinese and Western sources suggest that there are no dedicated tactical nuclear warheads, and so the figure for total nuclear warheads may actually be lower.

China's current strategic deterrent against the United States and European Russia is heavily dependent on a small, technically limited intercontinental ballistic missile (ICBM) force of DF-5 missiles. The land forces are silo-based at fixed sites, slow to fuel, less accurate, and have only one nuclear warhead per missile. This warhead has a very high yield. China's aircraft- and submarine-based forces are old, obsolescent, and rarely in use.

China's nuclear arsenal will expand in number of weapons and sophistication over the next ten to twenty years. Various agencies of the U.S. government have estimated that the likely increases will range from the "tens" to "75 to 100 warheads deployed primarily against the United States."[2] The two principal missile programs in this modernization effort will be the DF-31 and a follow-on, longer-range mobile missile, sometimes referred to as the DF-31A or DF-41. The mobile, solid-fuel DF-31 will have a range of 8,000 kilometers and carry a payload of 700 kilograms. It is expect-

---

[2]"Foreign Missile Developments and the Ballistic Missile Threat through 2015," available at http://www.cia.gov/nic/pubs/other_products/Unclassifiedballisticmissilefinal.htm.

ed that the DF-31 will begin deployments to replace the DF-3, perhaps by 2005. The development of the planned follow-on to the DF-31, the DF-31A, officially started in July 1986. This road-mobile, three-stage, solid propellant ICBM is expected to have a range of 12,000 kilometers, capable of striking targets throughout the continental United States. If development of this missile proceeds successfully, it may begin replacing the aging DF-5 force perhaps as early as 2010.

Given China's perceived need to counter a U.S. missile defense system, it is quite likely that the DF-31 and the DF-31A will have decoys and other countermeasures. The Chinese might also develop a multiple independently targetable reentry vehicle to counter a U.S. midcourse missile defense system. The payload capacity of the DF-31A will be lower than the DF-5 and will limit its capacity to carry countermeasures.

China may also try to develop a follow-on to the Xia-class nuclear ballistic missile submarine. The next generation submarine, designated the 094, would probably deploy sixteen of the new JL-2 submarine-launched ballistic missile (a variant of the DF-31), with a range of about 8,000 kilometers. Very little progress has been made, however, on the development of the Type-094 submarine, and the first of this class is unlikely to be launched before 2010.

China's no-first-use (NFU) doctrine on nuclear weapons is a manifestation of long-standing technological and political constraints on the PLA, and China is unlikely to abandon NFU at the strategic level in the near term. The modernization and expansion of nuclear capabilities may lead some parts of the PLA leadership to promote more flexible and technologically advanced doctrines. There have been discussions in some PLA writings of a more flexible "launch under attack" or "launch on warning" doctrine, and there are a few PLA analysts who express concern that the NFU policy will not deter a large-scale conventional attack or a conventional attack with weapons capable of mass destruction. Nonetheless, it remains difficult to change publicly Mao Zedong's axioms about nuclear weapons. Moreover, the NFU policy is designed to portray China's possession of nuclear weapons as defensive and just, while making a virtue of the reality of Chinese technological constraints.

Conventional Missiles

The development of significant numbers of conventionally armed short- and medium-range ballistic and cruise missiles is closely connected at present to the Taiwan situation. These missiles offer China its most potent form of coercive capability against Taiwan. There are currently three key conventional missile systems deployed by the Second Artillery: Dongfeng-15, Dongfeng-11, and the Dongfeng-21/25. The Second Artillery now uses global positioning systems to support midcourse and terminal guidance in order to increase accuracy and lethality. China currently has deployed approximately 350–400 short-range missiles opposite Taiwan, and the total number of missiles could rise to more than 600 by 2010.

The PLA appears to be developing a joint aerospace campaign for a possible Taiwan Strait scenario. This campaign could initially involve a barrage of short-range ballistic missiles targeting economic and critical infrastructures, followed by a PLAAF-led air campaign. A theater missile campaign would be an essential component of a broader denial campaign targeted at air, sea, and information capabilities and would aim to have a larger psychological effect on the Taiwanese leadership and populace.

During this type of campaign, the PLA would seek to damage runways, taxiways, weapons storage facilities, airfield command posts, and fuel depots to complicate the generation of sorties. The objective would be to shock and paralyze air defense systems to allow a window of opportunity for follow-on PLAAF strikes and rapid achievement of air superiority. PLA writings also prioritize strikes against naval facilities. Missiles could be used against naval bases, ground-based antiship missile facilities, and maritime command centers. Strikes supporting the quest for information dominance would target the civilian and military leadership, semi-hardened command-and-control centers, and key intelligence and electronic-warfare facilities. PLA conventional ballistic and land-attack cruise missiles would attempt to paralyze

Taiwan's command-and-control system by cutting off military forces in the field from the civilian and military leadership in Taipei.

America's technologically superior conventional theater-oriented strike assets present a severe challenge to China. Some PLA writings have suggested that a response to these capabilities is to use China's expanding short-range ballistic missile forces to strike U.S. forces and bases in Asia. Conventionally armed land-attack cruise missiles would also be an effective weapon for the Second Artillery, and new LACMs are currently being developed. The deployment of these missiles can probably be expected in the next several years.

Nuclear and Missile Forces: Continuing Issues

China's missile development, both tactical and strategic, will be very much affected by the development of missile defense by the United States as well as by the emerging U.S. nuclear doctrine. China will be modernizing its nuclear forces regardless of missile defense, but its nuclear force structure will certainly be configured in large part as a response to the missile defense of Taiwan, of U.S. theater forces, and of the U.S. homeland. Writings by Chinese military commentators make clear that China considers the American development and deployment of missile defenses, as well as a Nuclear Posture Review that encompasses a more flexible, capabilities-based nuclear doctrine, to be key measures of long-term U.S. strategic intentions. Missile defense will thus affect the Second Artillery modernization program at both the theater *and* the strategic level.

Central to any joint aerospace campaign directed against Taiwan is the question of how confident PLA and civilian leaders would be that this type of campaign could achieve its desired military and, more important, political objectives. How much certainty could Beijing have that the Taiwanese leadership or population would politically collapse under limited missile attacks? This type of attack could possibly prolong a campaign, but the air- and missile-driven, "rapid-war, rapid-resolution" coercive strategy is guided by the PLA's knowledge that it cannot sustain an air campaign. Air defense capabilities would be lost very rapidly, and, if fired all at once from their 120 launchers, the PLA's 400 SRBMs would provide only about three waves of missiles. By comparison, NATO's Operation Allied Force dropped a total of 23,000 munitions during the Balkan air operation of 1999.

Information Warfare
Information operations (IO), particularly computer-network operations, appeal to the Chinese military as an asymmetric weapon with a much longer range than conventional power-projection assets. The PLA believes the U.S. Department of Defense to be too dependent on civilian networks as well as on the NIPR-NET, the department's unclassified network. By attacking these networks, some Chinese analysts have suggested, the PLA would be able to degrade U.S. force deployments in Asia anonymously.

In the case of a Sino-U.S. conflict over Taiwan, Chinese military commentators have suggested that both the will of Taiwan to respond to PRC coercion and the ability of the U.S. military to intervene rapidly could be vulnerable to computer network attacks. These writings argue that the collapse of communication, financial, and power networks could cause widespread panic in Taiwan, thus putting pressure on the island's leadership to negotiate with the mainland. Some quarters in the PLA also appear to believe that computer network operations might be able to delay any U.S. military response sufficiently for PLA missiles, sabotage, and counterattacks to convince Taiwan to capitulate.

PLA writings consider IO a preemptive weapon to be used only at the opening phase of conflict. The PLA expects the enemy to make adjustments quickly to thwart any future IO efforts and thus for IO to be of little use in a protracted engagement. Though much of the PLA writings suggest the belief that potential adversaries are more information dependent than China, the highest priority in internal IO doctrinal writings is still the defense of Chinese computer networks. Only after this problem is addressed, the writings suggest, will the PLA contemplate tactical counteroffenses.

The PLA has begun to institutionalize and experiment with information warfare operations. China is sponsoring expert research in IO and the establishment of key centers of research and development. The expressed goal of these efforts is the eventual application of the theory to the battlefield. The PLA has not yet reached the phase of having a formal IO doctrine or the ability to operationalize the theory, but there is a great deal of effort on these fronts.

Information Warfare: Continuing Issues
The PLA is trying to develop IO capabilities. Much less clear is the PLA's level of operational capability for a computer network attack, as well as for the command-and-control of information operations. It is also worth noting that despite gains made by the PLA, IO is certainly a dimension in which the United States, and also probably Taiwan, hold an advantage over China. PLA writings, however, tend to overstate both the efficacy of U.S. IO capabilities and the vulnerability of U.S. computer networks. As PLA writings admit, China is vulnerable to attack. Moreover, Taiwan's Communications, Electronics, and Information Bureau is staffed with many of Taiwan's most able computer hackers.

The potential for misperception and conflict escalation should be considered. In its desire to develop tactics against either Taiwan or the United States, the PLA clearly hopes that an IO attack would be so difficult to attribute to China that the United States would be denied a proportional response. The PLA leadership may consider IO a low-risk option. In fact such attacks may lead to more rapid conflict escalation. Hence, assumptions about the ease, capability, or low risk of IO could lead to fundamental Chinese miscalculations.

PLA Budget
Chinese spending on military modernization rose throughout the 1990s. As announced in March 2003 at the National People's Congress, the official PLA budget stands at RMB 185.3 billion (U.S. $22.4 billion). This year's announced increase of 9.6 percent in military expenditures, however, was the lowest rise in thirteen years, and the official defense budgets remain relatively small in terms of their shares of gross domestic product (1.6 percent in 2002) and total government expenditure (8.5 percent in 2002).

Estimates by foreign analysts of the PLA budget vary between two to twelve times the published official figure. Higher estimates, $80 billion and upwards, tend to adopt a method of accounting (the use of purchasing power parity) that gives very imprecise results. The Task Force notes that actual expenditures are certainly higher than the official number. The published PLA budget excludes several important categories of spending, such as conversion subsidies; R&D costs; support of the People's Armed Police; the cost of weapons purchased from abroad; proceeds from PLA commercial ventures; PLA foreign arms sales revenue; and operations and maintenance costs that are shared by local civilian governments. In any event, dollar figures for military expenditures are hardly meaningful in a developing economy where the exchange rate is fixed by the government, where military personnel costs are not set by economic criteria, and where expenditures are so mixed between *renminbi*, the domestic currency, and imports that neither purchasing power parity—even if calculated separately for each class of expenditure—nor exchange rates are a good measure.

With this caution, the Task Force estimates Chinese defense spending may be closer to two to three times higher than the official number. This would place China's $44 billion to $67 billion in a range comparable to the $65 billion spent by Russia, the $43 billion spent by Japan, and the $38 billion spent by the United Kingdom.

The important issue for the PLA budget is not an imprecise dollar figure of uncertain meaning. It is rather the share of limited resources that the PRC leadership allocates to the military, the change over time in this share, and the overall military capability that these resources produce. The overall military capability produced determines the balance with U.S. capabilities. The share of limited resources allocated to the military sheds light, however dim, on Chinese strategic attitudes and general intentions—as the specific military capabilities give some sign of Beijing's specific intentions.

The Task Force notes that the PLA budget is becoming increasingly transparent—though there is disagreement as to how much—as formerly off-budget revenue items are being carried in the official budget. This shift, under the control of the Ministry of Finance, has been a factor in the overall official expenditure increases, particularly in 2001 and 2002. The Task Force is uncertain if the setting of the 2003 spending increase at 9.6 percent will be accompanied by a halting or a reversal of the trend of putting more actual expenditures in the official budget.

No matter what the trend, foreign arms purchases and some indirect R&D support are likely to remain off-budget and under the control of the Central Military Commission. Foreign arms purchases have averaged $700 million per annum from 1991 to 2000 but have risen sharply over the past three years, averaging $1.5 billion per annum (in part because of the cost of recent high-cost weapons systems purchases such as the Kilo-class submarines and the Sovremenny-class destroyers).

Analysis of the PLA budget illuminates the resources currently dedicated to force structure, personnel, equipment, and R&D priorities. China's 2002 Defense White Paper provides little concrete detail, asserting that 32 percent of official military expenditure was spent on personnel-related costs, while 34 percent was spent on operations and maintenance with an additional 34 percent on equipment. The Task Force believes it is important to note that China appears to budget a significantly large amount of money to the Second Artillery and its ballistic missile development.

China's defense expenditures are the product of a political process in which the PLA makes its claims on available public funds alongside nonmilitary claimants. Although there are currently no public "guns versus butter" disputes, the Chinese cannot be engaged in military modernization and economic reform without having questions about developmental priorities and budget allocations at the core of leadership debates. The expanding economy makes potential trade-offs easier, but these questions must still shade debate. The relative decrease in the 2003 budget may reflect such debates and competing priorities.

Military modernization is only one of several significant competing claims for resources and attention—others include social security, bank recapitalization, education, public health, science and technology, and large-scale public works projects. The leadership can only manage these claims by making trade-offs among different domestic interests all the time. The pressure to fund these competing claims is likely to increase within the next five years. The PLA is also likely to face other economic and educational bottlenecks, especially in labor markets, i.e., the low educational level of peasant soldiers and the need to compete with the growing private sector for college-educated and noncommissioned officers.

In spite of current PRC fiscal deficits and the enormous claims on government finance, the Task Force concludes that spending on force modernization and equipment purchases at approximately the rate seen in recent years is unlikely to cause unacceptable budget shortages for the next three to five years. A decline in defense spending is especially unlikely during this time period unless China's leaders conclude that they have acquired the necessary capabilities vis-à-vis Taiwan.

Chinese Defense Industry and Technology Issues
The Task Force's overall judgment is that (1) Chinese capabilities to develop, produce, and integrate indigenously sophisticated military systems are limited and likely to remain so for at least a decade; and (2) foreign acquisition will offset but fall well short of fully compensating for these domestic shortfalls.

Although the PRC has had some notable successes with defense production in the past—for example, the PRC engaged in serial production of fighters, rockets, and nuclear devices—Chinese defense industries have a poor record of providing the PLA with the necessary military systems, especially with regard to items related to a possible Taiwan scenario. The continued failure of the J-10 fighter program to move beyond the prototype stage may be only the most notable example—this fighter has been under development for more than two decades.

The continued reliance on foreign suppliers, especially Russia, not only for advanced weapons systems but also for repair and logistics is symptomatic of the weakness in China's own defense industrial base. Reliability of supply and maintenance capability and the difficulties of integrating foreign-sourced technologies into systems of systems are limitations inherent in relying on external suppliers. Chinese dependence on military equipment imports will persist for the foreseeable future, and an end to Russian arms sales and technology transfers would slow the pace of military modernization considerably. In any event, the Russia-China arms supply relationship remains limited. Russia is not transferring the means of production for weapons systems and end-use items or even for key component parts.

The imported weapons systems, from Russia as well as Israel and France (before the 1989 embargo), are a major improvement over what China had before, but most systems are of older, late–Cold War vintage. The SU-30s sold by Russia are of a significantly higher quality than anything China can produce on its own, and, although they may not be the state of the art, the Kilos are comparable with the submarines deployed by Japan and Australia.

China has been cut off from all U.S. and European military suppliers after an arms and defense technology embargo was imposed in 1989 in response to the Tiananmen tragedy. The Task Force judges that the continuation of the embargo is warranted because it will likely slow the pace of China's weapon modernization. A U.S.-only embargo, however, would have less impact. It follows that it should be a U.S. foreign policy priority to maintain common ground with other major arms suppliers, perhaps fashioned around a shared commitment not to enhance the PLA's power-projection capabilities, while maintaining an export control regime that does not unnecessarily harm U.S. commercial engagement with China.

The ability of Chinese defense industry enterprises to produce efficiently has been greatly limited by state ownership. Defense industry enterprises are overstaffed, in debt, unprofitable, and suffering from a declining product and customer base. There is a wide gap between producers and end users, and defense industries lack the managerial skills necessary for advanced systems integration.

Perhaps the greatest barrier to defense industry modernization is the bifurcation between civilian and military markets. PLA leaders criticize the defense industries for technological backwardness, failing to incorporate technologies from the civilian economy, being too geographically isolated in the western and central provinces, being poorly staffed, and suffering from overcapacity and duplication. The lack of management and system analysis skills continues to be a significant—if not the key—weakness in the defense industries.

There have been some notable improvements, however, in production and management since the political decision was made in the mid-1990s to hasten the modernization process in military industries. China is deficient in C⁴ISR, recognizes this weakness, and seeks improved capability through both internal development and imports. There have been recent advances in electronics and with the deployment of the new main battle tank. More important, the short-range ballistic missile program (DF-9 and DF-11), which in 1995 consisted of only a handful of launchers and a few dozen missiles, now includes several hundred highly capable missiles and over one hundred launchers.

Although there are weaknesses in key areas, China has an impressive and growing civilian science and technology base. In certain areas (e.g., telecommunications and electronics equipment) the Chinese capability is internationally competitive. But the ability of the Chinese to apply and integrate successfully these commercial technologies into their military capabilities is likely to remain problematic for at least the next decade. China is advancing less rapidly in developing military technology than in applying certain commercial technologies because the system of innovation and acquisition, unlike the civilian economy, remains the province of the PLA, the defense establishment bureaucracy, and state-owned enterprises whose productivity has lagged behind their nonmilitary and non–state-owned counterparts.

The development of a truly innovative indigenous technological base would be an extremely important development. Yet for this to have a direct impact on military modernization, the PLA would want to ensure that it had access to the most promising dual-use technologies as well as closer ties between defense industries and increasingly vibrant commercial enterprises. Indicators of these developments would include the creation of partnerships across the civilian and military sectors, the flow of management personnel from commercial to military industries and back again, and the development of a far more capable management and production system for translating technological advances into military applications.

China will maintain a passionate interest in acquiring military technology by all means: indigenous effort, import, and covert effort. The success of these efforts is uncertain, and the Task Force warns against overstating the significance to China's overall modernization of China's acquisition (by any means) of any single technology. The more critical issue is the Chinese ability to manage entire systems of systems, not its acquisition of individual components.

KEY UNCERTAINTIES

Although the Task Force does believe that U.S. forces could ultimately determine the military result of a direct conflict with China in any theater or at any level of escalation for at least the next twenty years, the outcome of any military conflict is never completely predictable. This uncertainty is heightened in the case of a potential conflict over Taiwan. Determining a "victor" in such a conflict would depend on political will in China, Taiwan, and the United States; Taiwan's military and political response; the U.S. military and political response; and public opinion in all three societies. In any case, the possibility that China could contest U.S. military influence successfully raises larger questions about the extent to which potential U.S.-China conflict could be contained, or might instead escalate to a wider geographic stage and to less restricted forms of warfare.

The Task Force spent considerable time discussing the situation across the Taiwan Strait, its role as a driver of Chinese military modernization, and its relationship to China's current and future strategic objectives. Some Task Force participants see China's approach to the Taiwan issue as a manifestation of a larger and more strategically ominous trend: the emergence of a China whose notions of regional expansion could put it on a collision course with American interests and commitments. Other participants, however, maintain a distinction between the Taiwan issue and the larger regional strategic interests called to mind by concerns over China as a "rising power" or potential "peer competitor" of the United States, and they challenge the assumption that a "great power" clash between the United States and China is all but historically foreordained. In either case, although the proper handling of the Taiwan issue cannot guarantee that a larger strategic confrontation between the United States and China will be avoided, the mishandling of the Taiwan issue could greatly accelerate movement toward such a confrontation.

The ability of the United States to influence the pace and scale of Chinese military modernization is also uncertain. Chinese military developments are substantially determined by what is happening within China, by the technical and financial resources available to the regime, and by Beijing's foreign policy priorities and external threat perceptions. Actions by the United States affect these perceptions, especially with regard to relations across the Taiwan Strait, the pace of U.S. military modernization, and U.S. missile defense plans.

The Task Force's projection about China as the predominant East Asian military power is based on the assumption that the other major regional powers—especially Japan—will continue their current military development trajectories. But an international or domestic crisis could fundamentally alter the security environment, threat perceptions, and defense spending of China's neighbors. Current events on the Korean Peninsula provide the most immediate example; a nuclear North Korea could strongly influence Japanese debates over revising Article IX of Japan's Constitution, the future size and role of the Japanese Self-Defense Forces, and the pursuit of a nuclear option that in turn would have major effects on Chinese military programs.

Current Chinese strategic objectives reflect a political consensus within the leadership. The recent leadership succession is unlikely to change core strategic goals at least in the near term, especially with Jiang Zemin retaining the chairmanship of the Central

Military Commission. That said, over the longer term, civil-military relations and the larger political context might change substantially. A liberalizing China may eventually have a more pacific foreign policy, especially in regard to Taiwan, but a China undergoing reform might also pursue its sovereignty concerns more confidently. Political instability might delay or derail military modernization; it might also provoke a diversionary military conflict as a way to restore domestic political support.

RECOMMENDATIONS

A detailed net assessment is beyond the scope of this Task Force, but it is clear that aside from a land war on the Chinese mainland, the People's Liberation Army (PLA) would be outclassed in a conventional war by the United States and will remain so well beyond this decade and the next. Given continued effort by the United States to stay ahead, the gap could continue indefinitely, although it is likely to narrow in a regional (although not global) context. However, China's purposeful development of capabilities directed toward a potential conflict over Taiwan and its apparently vigorous pursuit of short-range ballistic missiles and information warfare capabilities could prove to be exceptions to this broader generalization.

Recommendation 1: Monitor the development of specific capabilities in order to gauge the pace of Chinese military modernization.

The current trajectory of Chinese military modernization reflects the PLA's shift from a military with a continental orientation requiring large land forces for "in-depth" defense to a military with a combined continental and maritime orientation requiring a smaller, more mobile, and more technologically advanced "active peripheral defense" capability. The Chinese military is acquiring new weapons platforms and has reformed doctrine and training to allow the PLA to project power farther away from its shores and to defend those forward-deployed forces from various forms of attack, including aircraft, submarine, and missile.

As the PLA moves from its current capabilities toward its future aspirations, the Task Force recommends that the following key indicators be used to gauge the pace at which the Chinese military is modernizing. The indicators are grouped in five categories: command, control, communications, computers, intelligence, surveillance, and reconnaissance (C^{4}ISR); joint operations; precision strikes; combat support; and training.

C^{4}ISR

- Launch and maintenance of C^{4}ISR satellites able to provide real-time surveillance and expanded battle management capabilities
- Acquisition of airborne warning and control
- Development and use of unmanned aerial vehicles
- Development of Chinese information operations able to degrade U.S. intelligence, surveillance, and reconnaissance systems

Joint Operations

- Improvements in the ability to coordinate and execute multi-service exercises and joint operations in the various battle space dimensions (land, air, sea, electromagnetic spectrum, and outer space)
- Development of better air defense capabilities, including the integration of more advanced surface-to-air missiles (SAMs) like the SA-10
- The reorganization (or even abolition) of China's seven military regions (basically administrative entities) that would quickly enable the establishment of joint war zone commands (near equivalent of theater of operations in the U.S. military)
- Improvements in communication architectures that enable war zone commanders to coordinate the movements and actions of major units across current military region boundaries
- An increase in the number of command post exercises in which officers from different military regions and services practice joint command-and-control activities

Precision Strikes
- Improvement in targeting technologies, especially over-the-horizon targeting
- Development of stealthy, long-range cruise missiles
- Increased ability to use U.S., European, or future indigenous global positioning systems to the improve accuracy of short-range ballistic missiles (SRBMs) or other munitions
- Development and use of precision-guided munitions
- Training with antiship missiles by the People's Liberation Army Air Force (PLAAF) and/or the People's Liberation Army Navy–Air Force (PLANAF)
- Development of decoys, penetration aids, and other counters to missile defense measures

Combat Support
- Improvements to the recently established military region–based joint logistics system whereby it truly becomes capable of providing combat sustainability within the context of a war zone, not merely providing administrative peacetime logistic support within a military region
- Development of in-flight refueling and airborne command-and-control capabilities
- Moderate increase in airlift ability—beyond the three divisions in the airborne corps
- Moderate increase in sea-lift capabilities

Training
- Increases in the frequency of training missions with SU-27, SU-30, and other advanced aircraft; in the number of hours pilots train in advanced fighters; and in the sortie rates that can be generated with these aircraft
- Improved execution of training exercises that involve joint ground and air units

In addition, given China's critical dependence on Russia for weapons and defense technologies as well as spare parts, repairs, and logistics, the development of an indigenous capacity to manufacture the systems and weapons China now purchases from Russia would be an important sign of progress in Chinese defense industries. This is especially true in the case of technologies involved in fourth-generation fighters, over-the-horizon radars, air defense and air-to-air missiles, sophisticated surface combatants, and advanced submarines.

Recommendation 2: Look for signs that China's military development trajectory has changed significantly.

Although the Task Force has laid out the most probable development trajectory of the PLA over the next twenty years, it realizes that this trajectory may shift.

The Task Force developed the indicators listed in the previous section as a means to gauge the pace of a development trajectory focused on acquiring limited power-projection capabilities. The indicators that would represent major shifts away from these current priorities and would greatly change the nature of the Chinese modernization program, include:

- A crash program to build more amphibious warfare ships;
- Rapid expansion of the People's Liberation Army Navy (PLAN) marine force;
- Significant efforts to expand both airborne and airlift capabilities;
- Acquisition of SU-27s and SU-30s by the PLANAF or the expanded operation of PLAAF forces over water;
- The assignment of PLAN and PLAAF officers to senior PLA posts;
- A dramatic increase in the pace of submarine force modernization, including the construction and deployment of more Type-094 ballistic missile submarines;
- Major increases in intercontinental ballistic missile (ICBM) warheads by launcher numbers or by the development of multiple independently targeted reentry vehicles beyond those that might be necessary to maintain a Chinese nuclear second-strike capability in the face of U.S. missile defenses;
- Formal changes in the no-first-use (NFU) doctrine on nuclear weapons;

- Initiation of combat forces training in the use of nuclear or other unconventional weapons at the tactical level;
- Serious efforts to acquire or build one or more aircraft carriers;
- Greater attention, in doctrine and training materials, to the need to acquire a true "blue water" naval capability;
- The development of a proven capacity to conduct ballistic missile attacks against ships maneuvering at sea; and
- The development of a proven ability to disable U.S. space assets.

Domestic Change and Military Modernization

It is highly unlikely that Hu Jintao and other new leaders will challenge the general direction of Chinese security strategy in the next three to five years. However, the Task Force believes it is important to monitor how this new generation of leaders might try to ensure the support of the PLA in a future crisis and, conversely, how the PLA endeavors to maintain political support—and resources—for continued military modernization.

Any group of new Chinese leaders will have to protect their status as nationalists and as providers of economic growth and stability. Yet the balance between these two policy realms may change with new leaders. The new generation of leadership may focus on domestic stability and regime survival, which might translate into prioritizing economic policy and reducing social instability over a short- to mid-term solution of the Taiwan situation. On the other hand, new leaders with little foreign policy experience might also find their futures more closely tied to ending the perceived stalemate in the Taiwan Strait.

Reducing social unrest entails programs with great economic costs—improving the social welfare net, for example—that could require trade-offs between military spending and spending on other public policy projects. Tensions are possible between civilian leaders worried about pressing social needs and continuing economic reforms and a military frustrated that it may again be asked to defer making China a first-class regional power. Signs of this tension may be reflected in the PLA share of the national budget, in the tone of the media's PLA coverage and critiques of military spending, and in indirect, yet clearly identifiable, criticism of party activities and policies by senior PLA officers or authoritative PLA journals.

Political instability may delay or derail military modernization. In the face of a significant rise in domestic unrest (e.g., demonstrations and strikes; underground labor, religious, or political movements), the PLA might redirect resources from developing power-projection capabilities to those needed to exert internal control. Signs of shifting resources would be the interruption of training exercises and the redeployment of commanders and troops to support internal security organs.

The Task Force is divided as to whether a liberalizing China will mean a more pacific China. Most believe democracy will make China less likely to use force in resolving conflicts—especially Taiwan—but others do not take this position. Indicators of a liberalizing China include greater adherence to the rule of law, judicial reform, reversal of the Tiananmen verdict, release of political prisoners, expansion of village elections to higher levels of administration, removal of prohibitions against the transfer of residence from one location to another, continued diversification of Chinese media, growth of nongovernmental organizations and other aspects of civil society, and a diminution in control of Internet content. Other indicators of a liberalizing tendency in Chinese domestic affairs would include continuing pluralization of economic activity, reduction of the role of the state in the economy, and progress in establishing China's full adherence to the commitments defining the terms of its membership in the World Trade Organization, including transparency, nondiscrimination, reciprocity, elimination of trade barriers, and the protection of intellectual property rights.

Recommendation 3: Military-to-military dialogue should be broader and designed to achieve specific goals.

One of the central goals of military-to-military exchanges between the United States and China should be to increase Chinese defense transparency. Frank discussions between military organizations may not lower the level of suspicion among officers at the senior and lower levels of both the U.S. and Chinese militaries. Such dialogue, however, may reduce mutual misperceptions of intentions that could result in unintended conflict.

The United States should try to engage China in detailed discussions of Chinese doctrine and military planning, make thorough assessments of regional and global security issues, and hold discussions about the purpose and progress of PLA force restructuring and modernization. Specific departments of the PLA that should be engaged in these discussions include the General Staff Department Operations (Sub)Department, the General Armaments Department, the Second Artillery Command, the Academy of Military Sciences, and the military region headquarters. The United States should try to gain access to a wide range of ground, air, naval, nuclear, and command installations across China.

In addition to continuing the more routine military-to-military exchanges, the Task Force recommends that the U.S. government identify and initiate exchanges with influential published PLA authors. Many of the analysts who regularly interpret U.S. intentions and power in PLA newspapers and journals have never been to the United States or met an American military officer. Discussion between these authors and their American counterparts, based on their published writings, would be useful in reducing misperception and miscalculation on both sides.

The Task Force also takes particular note of the importance of utilizing openly published Chinese language materials on the PLA and its modernization, and calls for increased U.S. government support for efforts to collect, translate, and analyze PLA materials. From these materials, a number of analytical questions should be pursued: Among PLA sources, what are the more and less authoritative materials? What debates exist within the PLA and how meaningful are they? How different are PLA from non-PLA views on strategic issues? And who in the civil bureaucracy, think tanks, and society in general are likely to make arguments counter to some of the PLA's preferences and interests?

Recommendation 4: Initiate semigovernmental talks on crisis management issues.

Past acrimonious encounters between the United States and China over such issues as the accidental bombing of the Chinese embassy in Belgrade, Serbia, in 1999 and the collision of U.S. and PRC military aircraft near Hainan Island in 2001, as well as the possibility of even more serious encounters in the future over Taiwan, clearly suggest the need for both countries to improve the manner in which they anticipate or address potential or actual political-military crises. The United States and China should support the initiation of extended semigovernmental discussions designed to achieve such objectives. In this context, semigovernmental dialogue means talks between former officials, strategists, and scholars on both sides with the knowledge and support of their respective governments, but no action on behalf of their respective governments. Such talks would be relatively informal and unofficial, but with links to each government.

Recommendation 5: Enter into strategic dialogue with China over missile defense and nuclear modernization.

Over the coming years, China and the United States will need to wrestle with evolving perceptions (and misperceptions) of one another's strategic doctrinal shifts. The Task Force judges, in accordance with published CIA estimates, that China has straightforward means available to overcome the U.S. national missile defense now planned for deployment, and that China will do what is required to maintain and strengthen its own nuclear deterrent. Washington should state clearly and consistently to Beijing that U.S. missile defense plans are not aimed at China and that they neither signal hostile long-term intentions on the part of the United States toward China nor are they intended to negate a minimal Chinese deterrent.

The Task Force commends President George W. Bush's personal call to President Jiang Zemin to notify him of the U.S. intention to withdraw from the Anti-Ballistic Missile (ABM) Treaty and to express interest in holding strategic stability talks. But the Task Force believes more follow-up is necessary. The United

States and China should hold separate discussions on issues relating to nuclear strategic stability. Chinese interlocutors should include persons from the Second Artillery, the General Staff Department, General Armaments Department, and the Academy of Military Sciences.

The agenda for these discussions should include each side's nuclear modernization plans and nuclear doctrine, the basis of strategic stability in an environment that includes both offensive and defensive weapons, space warfare issues, and U.S. and Chinese missile defense programs. More specific questions that should be pursued include: How can China verify its NFU doctrine on nuclear weapons, and what does the PLA think about nuclear signaling?

Recommendation 6: Call for greater transparency in the PLA budget process.

Beijing's decision in the late 1990s to begin issuing Defense White Papers is a welcome development, and the latest edition (2002) shows modest progress in providing the most basic information about the PLA and the Chinese defense establishment. The Task Force suggests, however, that China could do much more by adhering to internationally recognized templates of defense spending (such as those of the Association of Southeast Asian Nations [ASEAN] Regional Forum, the UN Arms Register, NATO, the World Bank, the IMF, the Stockholm International Peace Research Institute, or the International Institute for Strategic Studies).

As mentioned above, U.S. government agencies' estimates of the size of the PLA budget vary widely. How estimates of Chinese military expenditures are arrived at is as important to the U.S. understanding of Chinese military trends as are the estimates themselves. The CIA estimates the size of the budget at somewhere between $45 and $65 billion.[3] Department of Defense estimates range from $65 billion to $80 billion.[4] Neither of these estimates has been

---

[3]Central Intelligence Agency, *The World Factbook 2002.*
[4]U.S. Department of Defense, *Military Power of the People's Republic of China: Annual Report to Congress* (July 12, 2002).

broken down, nor have the respective reports explicated their methodologies.

The Task Force believes that the U.S. government should mount a more disciplined effort to arrive at an estimate of various categories of the Chinese military budget and to acquire a more accurate picture of the Chinese military resource allocation process, with regard to both the PLA and the entire military budget. Unless a consensus can be reached as to what comprises the PLA budget, the "battle of estimates" loses much of its explanatory value and policy relevance.

Recommendation 7: Revisit the issue.

The Task Force stresses that estimating Chinese military capabilities beyond two decades is simply not feasible. Events will change the predicted course, and the United States should be prepared to respond accordingly. In sum, our report is not the last word on the subject. Rather, the report is an effort to create benchmarks. The Task Force will continue to monitor Chinese developments and, depending on circumstances, will reconvene to reconsider Chinese capabilities and U.S. policy.

ADDITIONAL VIEWS

The Task Force report is a very commendable effort to address both the overall state of military capabilities and milestones for policymakers to measure Chinese military power over the next two decades. It also makes a reasonable effort to address the short-term uncertainties and threats to American strategic interests in the region associated with Chinese programs and possible intentions regarding Taiwan. It is clear that any scenario that leads to the assertion of Chinese political control over Taiwan and a failure of the United States to effectively protect Taiwan from Chinese forcible assertion of direct sovereignty would have a dramatic impact on U.S. prestige throughout the region. As the report points out, "for U.S. policy toward China, this means maintaining the clear ability and willingness to counter any application of military force against Taiwan."

Consequently, the recommendation to continue to follow closely the evolution of Chinese military capabilities and leadership perceptions and intentions regarding Taiwan is of vital importance for U.S. strategic planning. Given consistently focused Chinese military acquisitions, deployments and operational planning, and training in regards to Taiwan, I believe the analysis should be for a shorter time frame, i.e., over a five to ten year period.

Of equal importance in minimizing surprise and miscalculation by the Chinese in the cross-straits situation is the need for far greater efforts by the U.S. government to engage the Chinese leadership in the creation of workable crisis management institutions, or so-called confidence-building measures. Here the Task Force recommendations seem to me to be weak. We recommend the institution of "semigovernmental talks on crisis management issues." However, the EP-3 incident cries out for renewed engagement at the highest levels for the development of such institutions, where, at a minimum, effective communication mechanisms are triggered whenever such incidents might occur. The U.S.-China Economic and Security Review Commission investigated U.S. attempts to build such institutions over several years and was dismayed to learn that the Chinese leadership rebuffed even the most modest of such efforts, leading to the inescapable conclusion that they have deliberately rejected crisis circuit-breaker mechanisms as a national policy regarding the United States. This is in stark contrast to the rather sophisticated and detailed crisis-management institutions negotiated, signed, and implemented over the last ten years by the Chinese with other states in the region, including India, Russia, and Central Asian Republics in the Shanghai Cooperation Organization as well as with ASEAN nations such as Vietnam, Thailand, and Laos. The lack of Chinese willingness to engage the United States at all should be cause for concern, and it would be useful for the Council to include an examination of this failure in subsequent Task Forces.

C. Richard D'Amato

This is a first-rate report—a detailed, thoughtful, and sophisticated summary of the views of the many independent and at times adamant Task Force members. I have no major objections to the findings of the report. My comments below deal with issues which I think need to be underscored, with which I am not in full agreement, or about which I am still somewhat ambivalent.

First, I want to underscore the importance of a methodological point made in the introduction. One has to be very careful not to leap from information about the evolving doctrinal and operational preferences of the People's Liberation Army (PLA) to inferences about the Chinese political leadership's foreign policy preferences. We would consider it an analytical mistake if the PLA's U.S.-watchers inferred U.S. foreign policy intentions solely from reading U.S. doctrinal manuals, training routines, and articles and books written solely by military officers. The policy discourse in Washington, I believe, has been all too quick to make this leap without demonstrating how precisely PLA doctrinal and operational concepts are related to the civilian leadership's political or long-term strategic intentions, to the degree that these exist.

Second, concerning the report's discussion of the Taiwan issue, I worry that the Task Force underestimates the degree to which the PLA thinks about and possibly plans for an outright invasion of Taiwan. I doubt this option would be considered under all political conditions. But one could imagine that in the face of an outright declaration of de jure independence (a declaration of a Republic of Taiwan, for instance), the Chinese leadership might consider an option that required the full subjugation of an independent regime as quickly as possible.

I agree with the report's conclusion about the need to balance deterrence and reassurance measures toward China and Taiwan. But at some point, the U.S. policy community needs to be more specific about what the worst fears of the Chinese and Taiwanese governments are and thus more specific about how both sides could be deterred from provoking the other and reassured that the other will not act provocatively. Specifically, the People's Republic of China (PRC) needs to be reassured that Taiwan will not declare formal independence in various forms (changing its flag, its official name, declaring independence from an entity called the Republic of China, among other possibilities), and Taiwan needs to be credibly assured that the PRC will not use force to compel unification. At the moment, it appears that military force alone is providing this deterrence/assurance. Chinese military power is clearly preventing a Democratic Progressive Party (DPP) government from adopting more formal symbols of independence. (It is unclear how much private U.S. messages to Taiwan help to prevent the DPP from "pushing the envelope.") And U.S. military power is clearly preventing the PRC from using force to compel unification. But the cost of these military disincentives is a burgeoning arms race across the strait and the concomitant instabilities and militarization of policies that this entails.

Thus, the report's language about how to balance the fears and interests of the PRC and the Republic of China (ROC) comes too close, it seems to me, to current official U.S. policy. Why should the United States not formally oppose a declaration of de jure independence, since the likely outcome of such a declaration would be war across the strait and, most likely, the end of democracy on

Taiwan? And how will democracy be preserved there in the face of a highly militarized and conflictual cross-strait environment? It is a mistake to conflate the two values at stake in this conflict—democracy on Taiwan and Taiwan's right to national self-determination. If the latter threatens the former (which is a realistic possibility in a highly militarized environment), it seems to me that Taiwan's formal self-determination is not a value that U.S. military power should be *currently* defending. The primary reliance on military power to deter the PLA's use of force reduces the credibility of whatever verbal assurances the United States supplies to "not support" Taiwan independence. This credibility decreases as U.S.-ROC military ties deepen and widen because, from Beijing's perspective, a de facto alliance is emerging—an alliance in which one of the partners (Taiwan) has a clear preference for de jure independence. Thus, there has to be a more concrete, specified conditionality, or strategic clarity, about the limits of actual U.S. military support in defense of Taiwan.

In addition, there has to be a shift from disincentives for the two sides of the Taiwan Strait to act provocatively to positive incentives to eschew provocative behavior. That is, are there credible commitments that the PRC and Taiwan can both make that would reassure the other that its worst fears would not materialize? To date, there seems to be a deficit of creative political efforts to search for these kinds of beneficial, positive incentives to eschew provocative behavior. As one example, China ought to allow Taiwan into all major international institutions as a nonsovereign state observer/participant. The institution should require only one condition from Taiwan, namely, that it loses its right to participate should it declare de jure independence from an entity called the Republic of China. This, then, offers the Taiwanese leaders a choice and a positive incentive not to declare de jure independence. Of course, such an offer from the PRC would have to be accompanied by a credible commitment not to use force to compel Taiwan's formal unification. To be credible, such a commitment would have to involve verifiable reductions in the size and capabilities of Chinese military deployments opposite Taiwan. Obviously, the political capital in China, Taiwan, and the United States that would be needed to implement these types of arrangements would be very expensive, but, after all, this is what political leadership is all about.

Third, on the question of China's own conception of its place in world politics, the report suggests that post–September 11 deployment of U.S. power in Central Asia and elsewhere led to a more sober assessment of the external security environment but that Chinese leaders continue to believe China's leverage over U.S. power continues to grow. I have my doubts about how widespread this belief is. There appears to be a growing acceptance in Beijing that China will operate in a unipolar, U.S.-dominated world for some time to come and that relative power trends are not necessarily in China's favor. The most recent estimate of China's comprehensive national power relative to the United States—this time produced by China's "CIA," the China Institute of Contemporary International Relations—is the most pessimistic about China's capacity to catch up to U.S. power, in striking contrast to earlier PLA studies of comprehensive national power.

Fourth, on the question of democratization and change in China's politico-military behavior, the Task Force members expressed two possibilities—that democratization would or would not make China less likely to use force. Presumably the former would change U.S. estimates of China's intentions, while the latter would not. I think this misses a third possibility—that democracy in China does not change its tendencies to use force, but that U.S. interpretations of these tendencies change. It seems highly likely that were Russia today still the Soviet Union, the United States would be much more hostile to Russian responses to the Chechnya problem than it currently is. A democratic China may not act more "benignly," but its behavior will likely be viewed as such by other democracies, thus lowering the degree of politico-military conflict between China and other democracies.

It is, of course, possible that a liberal, democratic China would actually be less likely to use force against its neighbors. This will depend on whose foreign policy interests are reflected by an increasingly responsive political leadership. That will, in turn, depend on the kind of transition to democracy China undergoes.

A militarized, nationalistic, populist regime born from social and political chaos would likely produce a more militarized foreign policy. On the other hand, a regime that incorporated the preferences of the emerging middle class and urban elite would probably produce a more liberal and internationalized foreign policy. The problem is that we know very little about the foreign policy preferences of Chinese citizens. Until we do, predictions one way or the other about the effects of democracy are likely to be highly speculative. What little we do know, on the basis of limited public opinion polling in China (in contrast to the journalistic impressions of rampant anti-Americanism and nationalism) is that foreign policy preferences are diverse and that wealth, education, and travel abroad are all positively related to a more "liberal," proto-internationalist world view (and higher levels of amity toward the United States). What the discussion in the Task Force suggests, therefore, is that a more informed debate about China's national security policies in the future requires more systematically collected data on public and elite opinion in China.

Fifth, concerning military-to-military relations and "socialization" of the PLA, I support this recommendation. However, we have to recognize that the PLA is, after all, a military. And like most militaries, its organizational socialization is primarily in a hard realpolitik world view; its mission starts with the assumption that diplomacy has more or less failed. The kinds of misperceptions that can be corrected through military-to-military exchanges are important ones, but any changes in these misperceptions will remain mainly in the realm of how the U.S. military operates, less so in terms of estimations of U.S. goals and intentions.

In the Chinese case, one source of misperception in the security policy process writ large is that the PLA has a perceived legitimate monopoly on national security policy. So, along with the need to "socialize" PLA (and U.S.) officers, security voices in China need to be pluralized. This would entail support for the development of an independent, civilian security expertise (even if, as in the United States, some of these voices are likely to be more hawkish than some military voices). Pluralization might also entail encouraging regional economic and political leaders to develop and articulate their own foreign policy and security interests. In the United States, regional economic interests with a large stake in the Chinese economy have been voices for moderation in Sino-U.S. relations. Thus, one research task is to identify how regional interests may differ from Beijing on certain security issues; whether these interests would stabilize or destabilize the Sino-U.S. relationship; and, if the former, how might they be encouraged? On the Taiwan issue, for instance, there is some evidence that political and economic leaders from eastern coastal China are less keen on coercive diplomacy. There are few channels for regional actors to develop and articulate their security interests. Perhaps U.S. consulates in China could be used to develop security dialogues with regional scholars and political and economic elites.

Finally, on the question of strategic nuclear dialogues between the United States and China, while I agree with the report that Washington should clearly state that U.S. missile defense is not designed to capture the Chinese deterrent, the credibility of verbal assurances depends on the state of political relations between the two sides. As former President Ronald Reagan famously noted, "Trust but verify." Why not invite Chinese inspectors to verify that the number of deployed interceptors does not exceed a number that would undermine China's deterrent? In addition, the Chinese could be allowed to place portal monitoring and other verification technologies at U.S. interceptor production sites to ensure that there is little chance of a U.S. missile defense "breakout" that might undermine China's deterrent.

Alastair Iain Johnston

I do not concur with the Task Force report's characterization of the appropriate U.S. policy toward Taiwan and the PRC that would reassure both parties "in a credible fashion that the worst fears will not materialize."

Taiwan scenarios probably play a central role in the PLA's modernization plans. As the Task Force report notes, however, Taiwan is fundamentally a political rather than a military issue, and current Chinese policy is to avoid a military confrontation if at all possible. As the Task Force report also observes, Chinese needs and priorities offer the United States the potential to influence diplomatically both Chinese plans for military modernization and policies relating to the threat of the use of force.

With respect to the Taiwan issue, this perspective suggests that the United States continue to make clear both to the PRC leadership and to the leadership on Taiwan that, consistent with the three communiqués and the Taiwan Relations Act, the United States (a) can support any peaceful resolution of the Taiwan issue that is agreed by both sides; (b) opposes any unprovoked attack on Taiwan; and (c) has not given Taiwan a "blank check" to pursue policies that would precipitate a crisis in the Taiwan Strait and drag the United States into a military confrontation with Beijing.

U.S. arms sales and related assistance to Taiwan should be guided by this approach. That is, our arms sales policy should strike the admittedly difficult and delicate balance between providing reassurance to Taipei with respect to (b) and reassurance to Beijing with respect to (c). Put differently, it should reassure Taiwan without provoking the PRC.

Arnold Kanter

U.S.-China relations are defined by a disturbing paradox. With no nation other than China does the United States have such a normal, even cordial relationship in so many areas—economic, social, currently political, educational—that coexists with a possibility of conflict that is so plausible, especially over a Taiwan scenario, that each side's military has contingency plans already on the shelf and has invested large amounts of human capital in thinking, planning, and war gaming to determine the best way to defeat the other.

But taking Taiwan out of the equation does not mean that future security relations between Beijing and Washington would be untroubled. Over the past six years, a quiet competition of ideas between the United States and China has been going on over what sort of security architecture will yield stability in East Asia. The United States argues that its alliance-based structure is and will be the basis for stability in the region for decades. (See the

"National Security Strategy" and "2001 Quadrennial Defense Review.")

China does not agree and in 1998, announced an approach that is at odds with the U.S. concept. This could be dismissed as a theological dispute if it were not so potentially destructive to U.S. strategy. Specifically, China continues to oppose bilateral military alliances. Chinese defense analysts argue that military alliances must be aimed at somebody, and they think that somebody is China. Beijing argues that in maintaining a system of alliances with Asian nations, the United States is following an outmoded "Cold War mentality." As a result, quietly and without a great deal of fanfare, China continues to attempt to undermine the foundation of U.S. security strategy in Asia—U.S. bilateral alliances—with its own "New Concept of Security." In the "2002 Defense White Paper," Beijing explicitly judges military alliances in Asia to be a factor of instability in the region.[5] I believe the United States is involved in a long-term "competition of security concepts" with China over how best to organize for regional stability.

This competition will undoubtedly collide with U.S. interests in the region. What the impact will be of China's attempts to undermine the very basis of our security strategy for the region is difficult to predict. So far, there is none. These ideas have not translated to a call from regional countries to discard bilateral alliances. This competition may never go beyond rhetoric and diplomatic competition, but it will nonetheless certainly introduce edginess to the long-term relationship.

Michael A. McDevitt

The annual report to Congress by the secretary of defense on Chinese military power in 2002 differs in focus and factual content in several important ways from our Task Force report. It is important to keep in mind while reading both reports that there are major uncertainties about Chinese intentions and capabilities. Some of these uncertainties are due to an extensive Chinese pro-

---

[5]Information Office of the State Council of the PRC, *China's National Defense in 2002* (Beijing: December 2002), p. 7.

gram of secrecy. Our Task Force recommends several new policies designed to reduce some of this uncertainty, but until the Chinese government is transformed into an elected, democratic regime, pervasive Chinese military secrecy will prevent the development of any real confidence about some fundamental aspects of Chinese military intentions and capabilities.

It should be understood that almost nothing in this Task Force report comes officially from Chinese government sources. China does not follow international standards of providing extensive details of its armed forces in official annual reports. On the contrary, China provides almost nothing of significance about its actual military power to the public. Some observers have noted that China's own senior civilian officials seem also to be kept in the dark about Chinese military affairs. Unfortunately, China has not been completely truthful about one of the rare facts it does make public—its defense budget. The defense spending figure that is provided by the Chinese military to the National People's Congress has been determined by our Task Force to be understated by at least half. Obviously, this Chinese military secrecy is troubling. Observers wonder what else is being concealed or is a subject for deception.

The 2002 report to Congress by the U.S. secretary of defense estimates the Chinese defense budget may even be twice as high as our Task Force estimate. In other words, the Pentagon suggests that China's claimed defense budget may be only one-fourth of its true value.

In the long term, if China continues this pervasive military secrecy, it may be self-defeating. Doubt already exists in Taiwan about China's claim to prefer to resolve the Taiwan dispute peacefully. Taiwan insists that no political settlement can occur until democracy comes to China. A secret military buildup focused on Taiwan can only further undermine progress toward a peaceful settlement.

Our Task Force has called attention to the danger of Chinese miscalculations about U.S. military power and resolve. There is no doubt that U.S. military power, in an abstract sense, is much greater than China's and will remain so for the foreseeable future.

This U.S. military superiority, however, is to some degree only in the eyes of the beholder. If Chinese military miscalculations and military secrecy make it impossible for China's leaders to assess correctly the costs of using force, U.S. superiority in our own eyes provides no guaranteed prevention of China causing a tragedy of epic proportions. We simply do not know how China assesses its own military power. It is not reassuring to read the many Chinese military writings about how the wily inferior force can always defeat the overconfident superior force as long as surprise and deception are employed. China's civilian leaders have no easy task in assessing the accuracy of the claims of their military leaders. Perhaps, a Chinese translation of our Task Force report will help them raise serious questions about their own military's exaggerated claims.

Michael Pillsbury

I believe the report pays insufficient attention to three factors that are shaping the scope, pace, and consequences of Chinese military modernization. Without fuller attention to these factors, any effort to devise a coherent, effective U.S. strategy to address the implications of China's military power will continue to fall short.

The first consideration is long-term U.S. defense strategy, and how America's increasing military-technological advantage will shape China's military modernization priorities. Like all major powers, China is assessing U.S. strategic predominance and the declared intention of the United States to maintain or even enhance its extant strategic advantage, as outlined in the September 2002 U.S. national security strategy document. The Chinese are seeking to balance their demonstrable requirement for stable, collaborative relations with the United States with the need to protect China's vital strategic interests against future shifts in U.S. policy that could pose a direct challenge to these interests. The areas of China's potential military development that would be most worrisome to the United States (specifically, future precision-strike capabilities, Beijing's ability to challenge U.S. maritime assets, and the PLA's information warfare activities) are all directly linked to American priorities and programs. As the report highlights, the Chinese are accelerating their modernization efforts in all three areas, and this is demonstrable cause for concern. But we cannot understand Chinese military modernization unless we first acknowledge that the PLA is responding to U.S. strategies and research and development activities, not embarking on a unilateral defense buildup.

The second consideration is whether the United States deems a more militarily powerful China an inherent threat to U.S. global or regional interests, and what the United States should do to forestall such a threat. The report implies that a measured pace of PLA modernization is acceptable to the United States, but an increased capability to coerce Taiwan is not acceptable. The report further advocates that the United States and Europe maintain the post-Tiananmen embargo on defense technology transactions with China, since this "will likely slow the pace of China's weapons modernization." It then asserts that the United States should agree with other major arms suppliers (presumably including Russia, which already ranks as China's principal source of advanced weaponry) to inhibit any further enhancement of the PLA's power-projection capabilities, while not impeding American commercial access to the Chinese market. I fail to see how these goals can be reconciled, especially given that (a) the Chinese are already developing these capabilities with substantial Russian involvement; (b) the most pressing Chinese need to enhance its power-projection capabilities is in systems integration, not in platform acquisition; and (c) an avowed technology denial strategy flies in the face of extant commercial realities affecting the U.S. corporate sector in the Chinese market. Finally, rather than inhibiting the flow of resources into China's future military development, a technology denial strategy will furnish the PLA with precisely the rationale it requires to demand more resources from the political leadership, not less.

The third consideration is the asymmetry between the report's advocacy of enhanced transparency on the part of the PLA (especially in its advanced conventional programs) and the absence of calls for equivalent reciprocity on the part of the U.S. military. To obligate the Chinese to far fuller disclosures on the entire spectrum of their military modernization priorities and activities, and to further seek extensive U.S. access to Chinese ground, air, naval, nuclear, and command-and-control assets, without an equivalent commitment on the part of the United States, will go nowhere. It will also reinforce recurrent Chinese suspicions about the underlying purposes of enhanced military-to-military relations. By contrast, the report acknowledges the need for both countries to undertake a shared assessment of their respective priorities in missile defense and strategic nuclear modernization, so as to reduce misperceptions and (quite possibly) to avoid needless resource commitments that would be in neither state's interest. An equivalent approach should govern discussions on the modernization of conventional forces: there needs to be a mutual, interactive process of information disclosure, not one-sided transparency. Without such openness on the part of the United States, the Chinese will have few incentives to provide the reassurance that the U.S. purports to seek, and the PLA will revert to long-standing habits of dissemblance, nondisclosure, and information denial that do not advance the goal of productive, maturing military-to-military relations.

Jonathan D. Pollack

TASK FORCE MEMBERS

KENNETH W. ALLEN is a Senior Analyst in "Project Asia," the Asian security studies center at the CNA Corporation. He served twenty-one years in the U.S. Air Force, including assignments in Taiwan, Japan, China, and Headquarters Pacific Air Forces.

DESAIX ANDERSON is a writer and artist. He served as Executive Director of the Korean Peninsula Energy Development Organization as well as Principal Deputy Assistant Secretary of State for East Asia, covering Japan, China, and Korea.

PAUL BRACKEN is a Professor of Management and Political Science at Yale University.

HAROLD BROWN, Chairman of the Independent Task Force on Chinese Military Power, is a Partner at Warburg Pincus and Counselor at the Center for Strategic and International Studies. He served as Secretary of Defense during the Carter administration and was the first Secretary of Defense to visit the People's Republic of China (in 1980).

THOMAS J. CHRISTENSEN is a Professor of Political Science at the Massachusetts Institute of Technology.

BERNARD D. COLE is Professor of International History at the National War College. He previously served for thirty years in the U.S. Navy.

RICHARD N. COOPER is Maurits C. Boas Professor of Economics at Harvard University. He previously served as Chairman of the National Intelligence Council and was Under Secretary of State for Economic Affairs.

Note: Task Force members participate in their individual and not institutional capacities.

C. RICHARD D'AMATO* is Vice Chairman of the U.S.-China Economic and Security Review Commission, a former delegate in the Maryland General Assembly, and a retired Navy Reserve Captain. He previously was Foreign Policy Director for the Senate Democratic Leader and Staff Director for Senators Abraham Ribicoff and Jim Jeffords.

JOHN DEUTCH is Institute Professor at the Massachussetts Institute of Technology. He previously served as Director of Central Intelligence, Deputy Secretary of Defense, Under Secretary of Defense for Acquisitions and Technology, and Under Secretary of Energy.

WILLIAM H. DONALDSON† is Chairman of the Securities and Exchange Commission. He co-founded Donaldson, Lufkin & Jenrette, is a past Chairman and CEO of the New York Stock Exchange, and served as Under Secretary of State for Security Assistance in the Nixon Administration.

JUNE TEUFEL DREYER is Professor and Chair of the Political Science Department at the University of Miami, Coral Gables, and a Senior Fellow at the Foreign Policy Research Institute. She is currently a Commissioner of the U.S.-China Economic and Security Review Commission.

DAVID M. FINKELSTEIN is the Director of "Project Asia" at the CNA Corporation. A retired U.S. Army China Foreign Area Officer, he served in multiple China-related assignments throughout his career, including Assistant Defense Intelligence Officer for East Asia and the Pacific in the Pentagon, on the Joint Staff, and teaching Chinese history at West Point.

THOMAS S. FOLEY is a lawyer with the firm Akin, Gump, Strauss, Hauer & Feld and a former U.S. Ambassador to Japan. Prior to becoming Ambassador, he served in Congress from 1965 to 1994.

---

* Individual largely concurs with the report but submitted an additional view.

† Mr. Donaldson participated as a member of the Task Force until his appointment as Chairman of the Securities and Exchange Commission in February 2003.

JOHN FRANKENSTEIN is a Research Associate and adjunct faculty member of the Weatherhead East Asia Institute, Columbia University.

BATES GILL holds the Freeman Chair in China Studies at the Center for Strategic and International Studies.

BONNIE S. GLASER has served as a consultant on Asian affairs for the U.S. government since 1982. She is a Senior Associate at the Center for Strategic and International Studies and at Pacific Forum, CSIS.

JOHN L. HOLDEN is President of the National Committee on U.S.-China Relations. He was based in Beijing and Hong Kong for fifteen years while doing business in China.

ALASTAIR IAIN JOHNSTON* is the Governor James Albert Noe and Linda Noe Laine Professor of China in World Affairs at Harvard University.

ARNOLD KANTER* is a Principal and founding member of the Scowcroft Group. He served as Under Secretary of State from 1991 to 1993 and is currently a member of the President's Foreign Intelligence Advisory Board.

ROBERT A. KAPP is President of the U.S.-China Business Council, the principal organization of U.S. companies and firms conducting trade and investment with China.

CHARLES R. KAYE is Co-President of Warburg Pincus.

MICHAEL KREPON is the founding President of the Henry L. Stimson Center. His most recent book is *Cooperative Threat Reduction, Missile Defense, and the Nuclear Future* (Palgrave, 2003).

NICHOLAS R. LARDY is a Senior Fellow at the Institute for International Economics.

DEBORAH M. LEHR is Chairman of MBP Consulting and previously served as Deputy Assistant U.S. Trade Representative at the U.S. Trade Representative Office and Director for Asian Affairs at the National Security Council.

KENNETH G. LIEBERTHAL is Professor of Political Science and William Davidson Professor of Business Administration at the University of Michigan. He previously served as Special Assistant to the President for National Security Affairs and Senior Director for Asia at the National Security Council.

WINSTON LORD is Co-Chairman of the International Rescue Committee. He previously served as Assistant Secretary of State for East Asian and Pacific Affairs in the Clinton administration, Ambassador to the People's Republic of China in the Reagan and Bush administrations, and President of the Council on Foreign Relations.

MICHAEL A. MCDEVITT* is Director of the Center for Strategic Studies at the CNA Corporation and founder of CNA's "Project Asia." A retired Rear Admiral, he served in Asia policy positions in the Office of the Secretary of Defense and as J-5 at Pacific Command.

JAMES C. MULVENON is the Deputy Director of the RAND Center for Asia-Pacific Policy.

MICHAEL PILLSBURY* is a consultant to the Defense Department, a research affiliate at the National Defense University, and a Councilor of the Atlantic Council. He formerly served as Assistant Under Secretary of Defense for Policy Planning and as Special Assistant for Asian Affairs in the Office of the Secretary of Defense.

JONATHAN D. POLLACK* is Professor of Asian and Pacific Studies and Director of the Strategic Research Department at the Naval War College.

---

* Individual largely concurs with the report but submitted an additional view.

JOSEPH W. PRUEHER, Vice Chairman of the Independent Task Force on Chinese Military Power, is a Consulting Professor and Senior Advisor on the Stanford-Harvard Preventive Defense Program. He previously served as U.S. Ambassador to China; is a retired Navy Admiral; and was formerly Commander in Chief, U.S. Pacific Command.

ERVIN J. ROKKE is President of Moravian College. He is a retired Lieutenant General and former President of the National Defense University.

ROBERT S. ROSS is a Professor of Political Science at Boston College and a Research Associate of the John King Fairbank Center for East Asian Research at Harvard University.

J.S. ROY is Managing Director of Kissinger Associates, Inc. He previously served as Assistant Secretary of State and U.S. Ambassador to China.

ANDREW SCOBELL is Associate Research Professor and a specialist on Asia at the Strategic Studies Institute of the U.S. Army War College.

ADAM SEGAL, Director of the Independent Task Force on Chinese Military Power, is the Maurice R. Greenberg Senior Fellow in China Studies at the Council on Foreign Relations.

DAVID SHAMBAUGH is Professor and Director of the China Policy Program in the Elliott School of International Affairs at George Washington University and a nonresident Senior Fellow in the Foreign Policy Studies Program at the Brookings Institution. He is presently on leave as a 2002–2003 Fellow at the Woodrow Wilson International Center for Scholars in Washington, D.C.

SUSAN L. SHIRK is a Professor in the Graduate School of International Relations and Pacific Studies at the University of California, San Diego, and Research Director at the Institute on Global Conflict and Cooperation. She also served as Deputy Assistant

Secretary for China, Taiwan, and Hong Kong in the Bureau of East Asian and Pacific Affairs at the U.S. Department of State from 1997 to 2000.

WALTER B. SLOCOMBE[††] is a member of the Washington, D.C.-based law firm, Caplin & Drysdale. He served as Under Secretary of Defense for Policy from 1994 to 2001 and was Principal Deputy Under Secretary for Policy from 1993 to 1994.

KAREN SUTTER is Director of Business Advisory Services at the U.S.-China Business Council. She previously served as the Director of the Atlantic-Pacific Program at The Atlantic Council of the United States.

MICHAEL D. SWAINE is a Senior Associate at the Carnegie Endowment for International Peace and Co-Director of CEIP's China Program. He was formerly a Senior Political Scientist and the first recipient of the Asia Research Chair at RAND.

G.R. THOMAN is a Managing Partner of Corporate Perspectives, LLC. He managed Chinese businesses in four companies as a former CEO of Xerox and a former Group Executive of IBM, Nabisco Foods, and American Express.

LARRY D. WELCH is currently the President and Chief Executive Officer of The Institute for Defense Analyses in Washington, D.C. Before assuming his current position, he served for thirty-nine years in U.S. military forces, from private in the U.S. Army National Guard to Chief of Staff, U.S. Air Force.

DONALD S. ZAGORIA is Project Director of the U.S.-China-Taiwan Relations Program at the National Committee on American Foreign Policy.

[††]Mr. Slocombe participated as a member of the Task Force until his appointment in May 2003 as Senior Security Advisor (Ministry of Defense) of the Coalition Provisional Authority in Iraq.

TASK FORCE OBSERVERS

LIST OF ACRONYMS

AAM	Air-to-Air Missile
ABM	Anti-Ballistic Missile
ASEAN	Association of Southeast Asian Nations
C⁴ISR	Command, Control, Communications, Computers, Intelligence, Surveillance, and Reconnaissance
DPP	Democratic Progressive Party
DPRK	Democratic People's Republic of Korea
ICBM	Intercontinental Ballistic Missile
IO	Information Operations
LACM	Land-Attack Cruise Missile
NCO	Noncommissioned Officer
NFU	No-First-Use
PLA	People's Liberation Army
PLAAF	People's Liberation Army Air Force
PLAN	People's Liberation Army Navy
PLANAF	People's Liberation Army Navy–Air Force
PRC	People's Republic of China
R&D	Research and Development
ROC	Republic of China
ROTC	Reserve Officer Training Corps
SAM	Surface-to-Air Missile
SARS	Severe Acute Respiratory Syndrome
SRBM	Short-Range Ballistic Missile